THE
COMPLETE
Holiday
ORGANIZER

THE COMPLETE Holiday ORGANIZER

E·M·I·L·I·E BARNES

HARVEST HOUSE PUBLISHERS
Eugene, Oregon

THE COMPLETE HOLIDAY ORGANIZER

To my Bob for encouraging me to be the woman God wants me to be. Your loving support over the years helped me to use my creativity in making our home a warm and happy place to live.

To our children, Jenny and Brad; our son-in-law, Craig, and our grandchildren, Christine, Chad, and Bevan, who laugh with me and not at me. We've had some beautiful memories and started warm traditions together.

The warmest strokes I get out of my life come from my Lord and from all of you. Thank you.

To a very talented friend—Sheri Torelli—who has spent hours of loving time typing all our manuscripts with a happy heart.

My love and blessings to all of you because His joy is in our hearts.

Contents

Introduction

There was no Christmas, no tree, no parties, no gifts, no cookie exchange, no ornaments hung or given, no excitement, no wish list—just one little girl looking out a window, longing to be involved in the most beautiful season of the year.

I was raised in a Jewish home. Yes, there was love, there was food, and there was Hanukkah. I was different but I wanted to be like everyone else, enjoying Christmas carols, Christmas shopping, Santa, sleigh bells, reindeer and, most of all, Christmas traditions.

I was 11 when my father died. My mother became even stronger in the Jewish faith and I went weekly to Hebrew school and Temple. It wasn't kosher to celebrate Christmas. God, however, had other plans for my life. God brought a young man into my life who did have Christmas, did believe in Jesus as Messiah, and did celebrate all the beautiful traditions of the Christmas holiday. My heart was touched by Christ's love as Bob shared the true Christmas story with me one evening: that God did have a Son, His name is Jesus, and He is the Messiah our people are waiting for. "I am the way, and the truth, and the life; no one comes to the Father but through Me" (John 14:6). "I came that they might have life, and might have it abundantly" (John 10:10).

Bob's Christian heritage and upbringing surfaced strongly during those early dating months and, through his loving influence, I received Christ into my heart and became a believing Christian. We were married a year later, and I'll never forget our first Christmas together—for me the very first Christmas of my life. Money was short but we had a tree and gave each other ornaments which became a tradition for our family.

9

INTRODUCTION

When our daughter Jenny married Craig, one of the wedding gifts we gave them was 22 ornaments of Jenny's from over the years. It was a great beginning for their first Christmas tree together and they since have continued the tradition.

Our son Brad dated a Jewish girl in high school. She watched us trim our house with lights, bring the tree in the living room, set it in place, put the Christ-centered wreath on the front door, and wrap packages. It took me back to my childhood days of looking through the windows and watching families celebrate a holiday I wasn't a part of. That year Brad invited his girlfriend to share with us our tradition of tree-trimming. I'd always make it a special time around the tree. I'd fix an easy meal around the coffee table of "build your own Mexican tree" (tostadas), Sloppy Joes, bean soup, or hamburgers.

Bob and I would wrap the children's ornaments in brown paper sacks with their name written on the outside and a bow on top. So we did the same for Cheryl, Brad's friend. There was a lot of eating and talking. We'd have Christmas music going and pretend it was cold or snowy outside. (In Southern California you have to do all you can to make it seem like winter.)

I wish you could have seen the joy in Cheryl's eyes when she opened her ornament and, with an almost reverent attitude, placed hers on our tree. Cheryl was with us for the next three years and enjoyed our tradition. I prayed, "Lord, someday let Cheryl take these ornaments and put them on her own tree. God has answered that prayer because, in her senior year in college, she did receive Christ as Messiah and is now experiencing the abundant life in Christ.

Christmas can and should be a holiday we look forward to. Today our busy lives are so filled with stress and schedules to meet that we often tend to dread the holidays instead of treasuring them.

This book is written for those who want to have a stressless Christmas—a Thankful Thanksgiving—a Heartfelt Valentine's Day—Beautiful Birthdays—and Ecstatic Easters.

The commercialism of these holidays has reduced the joy and real meaning of many of them. Our great-grandparents knew

INTRODUCTION

what to do with little or nothing to make holidays special and memorable. With organization and the creative suggestions in this book, you too can make a hectic holiday into a treasured memory.

Learn to Create
Treasured
Holiday Memories

1

Learn to Create Treasured Holiday Memories

In our hectic stress to make a living and meet all the time demands upon our 24 hours per day, we are too exhausted to spend quality time together to create treasured holiday memories. When these days come, we just want to lay back and do nothing. It's kind of a catch-up day in order for us to be ready to start again. We continually ask, "How do I get off this treadmill?" You have to do it on purpose—learn to create treasured memories! They don't happen by chance. For the family to endure today, we have to plan for success. Take time to live life with a purpose.

I want to give special encouragement to Mom and Dad to work together as a team to make life meaningful. Children love to see their parents working with a plan. If Dad is reluctant to get involved, then Mom will have to carry the extra load to live life with a purpose. Planning ahead for holidays will also give single parents an extra spurt of energy for living life with a quality of memories.

You don't need money to create memories, you just need a desire. As adults, many of our memories are from our childhood or from when we were first married. Looking back to our early married life, Bob and I had very little money, but we look back with fond memories. Now we have much more financial independence, but our early memories are still very vivid. Someone shared with me once, "Successful people do what unsuccessful people aren't willing to do." That statement had a real impact on my life. From that day on I began to identify what those things were. One that was brought to mind was that successful people planned their lives and I wasn't planning my life very well at that time. Since then, I've learned to create treasured holiday memories.

Deuteronomy 6:6,7 states, "And these words, which I am commanding you today, shall be on your heart; and you shall teach them diligently to your sons and shall talk of them when you sit in your house and when you walk by the way and when you lie down and when you rise up." This Scripture made it clear to Bob and me that we were responsible to teach our children the important issues of life. We couldn't depend upon the schools, churches, Sunday schools, Christian conference camps, or any other agencies. It is up to the family and its members to teach, learn, and hand down from one generation to the next those values that are cherished. As we get older and balance out the successes of our lives, we realize there are two important questions to answer: What did I do with God? and What did I do with my family? If we can answer each question positively, we can feel that we have lived life with a purpose.

Let's start with first things first: "But seek first His kingdom and His righteousness; and all these things shall be added to you" (Matthew 6:33). Each day we need to make the commitment to establish God as number one in our lives. If you have not made the decision to give God the number-one spot in your life, do so today; settle that basic question.

By reading this book you have started with priority number two: your family. Live a day at a time, but live that day with a plan. May God direct you and your family as you begin to create treasured holiday memories.

Birthdays

2

Birthdays

Thus it came about on the third day, which was Pharaoh's birthday, that he made a feast for all his servants. . . . (Genesis 40:20).

When Observed: On the person's date of birth.
Earliest Observance: Pharaoh in Genesis 40:20

The practice of marking an individual's exact date of birth came into existence only with the recording of time by a fixed calendar. Originally birthdays were not celebrated by commoners. It has only been in recent times that general populations have celebrated individual birthdays.

In Europe and America an individual's birthday is celebrated with a family dinner or a party with friends and the customary giving of gifts. This is an important occasion, especially for a child.

Different countries share different traditions from our standard observances. In general, this is a specific time each year to give special praise and recognition to the person whose birthday we celebrate. One way to make this a special tradition in our families is to take time out of our busy schedules to do something different.

This is your day!
Good news! Psalm 139:13–16

You created every part of me; you put me together in my mother's womb. I praise you because you are to be feared; all you do is strange and wonderful. I know it with all my heart. When my bones were being formed, carefully put together in my mother's womb, when I was growing there in secret, you knew that I was there—you saw me before I was born. The days alloted to me had all been recorded in your book, before any of them ever began. (TEV)

Birthdays are always made special in our home. Maybe because when I was growing up they never were. I remember when I was 12, I gave myself my first birthday party. My mother was trying to make ends meet after my father's death by opening a small dress shop. Even though we lived in three rooms behind the store, mother was busy with customers, doing alterations and book work. Birthday parties were not a priority. I always wanted a party, so I did it myself. I gave out invitations, cleaned the house, baked a cake, cut flowers, and put up streamers. My friends came and brought presents. I was so embarrassed I hid in the closet and wouldn't come out. The adult in me could plan it, organize it, and create it, but the little girl couldn't handle it. I'd never had such attention. I wanted it, but when it came it was overwhelming. It was probably then that I decided to make birthdays special for my children someday.

Many times during the year we'd talk about our birthdays— I'd always, and still do, make the children's favorite meal. Most every year they had a party of some kind.

I'll never forget when our Jenny had her seventh birthday. Of any of us in the family, Jenny loved a party the most and she still does even though she is a grown woman with three children of her own. We planned for her to invite ten of her closest friends from church and school. She took her invitations and hand carried them to each person—but unknown to me, she not only invited her ten friends but any child who even looked like a friend. The mothers started dropping off their children for the party. We ended up with 24 children. The 12 cupcakes we cut in half and the children scrambled for the prizes. It was crazy but that was our Jenny. She couldn't hurt the other children's feelings by not inviting them, so she invited her whole class. It was most definitely a party and truly a memory for Mom.

Parties with themes can be a lot of fun and will flow well

because you have a definite plan. When my Bob turned 50, we had a surprise fiftieth BEARthday Party—our theme was teddy bears. The invitations were teddy bears cut out of brown construction paper and said, "YOU'RE INVITED TO BOB'S 50th BEARTHDAY. Bring a teddy dressed in costume to depict Bob."

The plans took quite a while and when I got home, Bob was really upset that I had been gone so long. "Where have you been? The phones have rung off the hook, the UPS delivery came. People came by for orders. It's really hard for me to handle all this by myself." Well I couldn't tell him the truth or I'd give the whole surprise away. But I sure wanted to say, "I was at Jenny's making and mailing YOUR birthday invitations. He never caught on and it was a surprise.

I filled the room with helium balloons tied to each chair. The centerpiece consisted of a potted plant with small cloth teddy bears I had made and stuffed with fiberfill then glue-gunned onto a bamboo spear I purchased from the Oriental section of the market. So they became teddy plant sticks. I tied three balloons on the handle of the plant baskets. A friend made baseball hats with a teddy bear on the bill for each man (25). I had silk-screened on white T-shirts for the men and women a big teddy bear with "Bob's 50th BEARthday 1984" which everyone wore to the party.

The high school where our children attended had as their mascots two Poly Bears. So Jenny, being a cheerleader, called the school and asked if we could borrow the two mascots for Bob's BEARthday party. They felt it was an honor to be invited. So we had bears all over the place. When Bob arrived at the party, the two Poly Bears slipped out to escort him in carrying a dozen helium balloons. I wish I had a video of that scene. It was GREAT!!! In they came. We all yelled, "Surprise BEARTHDAY, Bob!" But that was just the beginning.

After dinner and honey buns, each couple stood up with their dressed teddy bears and explained why they dressed it that way. All depicted different qualities of Bob's friendship. We had the Preppy bear wearing saddle shoes. Bob most generally wears saddle shoes. We had the football referee with a black-and-white shirt and a whistle around his neck. Bob spent many years refereeing Pop Warner and high school football games to supplement our salary. We had a teddy studying his Bible wearing glasses. Bob has taught adult and college Bible studies most of our 32 years of marriage. Our daughter and son-in-law brought a gray-haired Papa bear wearing glasses since they have made Bob a grandpa the children call Papa Bob. On and on the display of teddy bears came.

A long-time friend, Bob Swanson, wrote Bob a song and entertained the guest with his guitar music and song. We all nearly keeled over with laughter. The local newspaper got wind of the affair and came and took pictures and wrote an article which all of Riverside viewed the next week. so the whole world knew Bob Barnes had turned 50. It was GREAT and a memory to last a lifetime.

Our daughter gave her husband a surprise birthday party the first year they were married and everyone came dressed in pink—even the men wore pink shirts. It was a simple thing to do and yet it made the party a bit different and very creative.

Here's an idea for the working woman. I went to a surprise 40th birthday party for my friend Yoli Brogger. We all met at 5:00 A.M. at her neighbor's home dressed in our nighties and robes. The working gals put robes over their clothes. We walked down the middle of the street with dawn barely on the horizon, through her front door, down the hall into their bedroom and yelled "Surprise!" She was in shock—hair tossled, no makeup. She thought it was a dream as 20 silly mid-life ladies stood at her feet and sang "Happy Birthday." We had such a fun time drinking tea and coffee with birthday cake and fruit at 5:30 A.M. By 7:00 A.M. the presents were opened and the party over.

Another of our friends had her surprise birthday party for 40 days before she turned 40. That party celebration went on for 40 days with lunches and brunches for a much-loved gal.

Birthdays don't have to be a surprise. Our son Brad isn't so big on birthday parties as such. He enjoys quiet family times with favorite foods and warm conversation. We acknowledge that and occasionally have a small party for him.

Other birthday ideas that might enrich your day:

1. *Birthday flag or banner*—Design and create a birthday flag or banner for each family member. Make this flag or banner out of cloth that will last (canvas is great). Place on it the person's favorite colors, sports interests, school activities, hobbies, etc. Either fly the flag on a pole or hang the banner from a special hook on a fence or on the side of the house. You might even have a special ceremony to sing a song, yell a yell or dance a dance to start the day off right.

2. *Birthday cup and/or plate*—Designate a special cup and/or plate to be used by the members of your family only on their birthday. A great way to give special honor and recognition to that birthday person.

3. *A song at 9:02 A.M.*—On June 8th, I was born at 9:02 A.M. and at the exact time each year my family sings "Happy Birthday" to me. Even in college, I was sure to be in the dorm at that exact time, because I knew I would receive that traditional call. Even today, though married and living in another state, I still look forward to that traditional call. I now have started that same tradition with our two sons.

4. *Love notes for Daddy*—While baking Dad's favorite German chocolate cake one year, we decided to do something special for him. We wanted to give him a gift that would last all year. We took small strips of paper and wrote a message that Dad could cash anytime during the year. We placed these in a small colorful tray that could set on his dresser. We wrote things like:

Good for one back rub—Jenny

Good for one fried chicken dinner—Mom

Good for one extra hug and kiss—Brad

5. *A special beginning*—Plan special activities for the birthday honored guest. Some might be:

- Choose one gift and put it at the birthday person's place at the breakfast table to be opened as soon as their day begins.
- Have the birthday person plan the menu for supper (or you might even let the person choose a special restaurant if budget permits).

- Have a tape cassette reserved just for the birthday person. Each year interview the person regarding special events and occasions during the last year: sad times, fun trips, friends, etc. Listen to the previous years' interview before adding the new segment.
- Have clean linens on the bed and clean towels in the bathroom.

6. *Weekend celebration*—Try to celebrate your children's birthday at a neat hotel that has a pool, game room, and nearby restaurants. Just getting together as a family brings home many fond stories to go into the memory bank.

7. *Creative gifts*—
Tickets to the zoo, or a film
A beach towel
New socks
Art supplies

8. *Un-birthday party*—Pick a date during the warm summer months and have a party with all the birthday trimmings. Who is it for? No one special, just a cause for family and friends to get together.

9. *Adopted birthday*—If you have an adopted child, you might want to let that child have two birthdays. One for their actual birthday, and another celebrating the day on which they came into your home. This second day makes that child feel special as a part of a very special family.

10. *Have a happy "half" birthday*—Make a big deal celebrating your child's half birthday. You can carry out the theme by having a "half" birthday cake, a "half" glass of punch, "half" of a birthday card, etc. Be creative in carrying through the "half" theme.

Birthday Letters in a Shoe Box

When I was 21, my mother presented me with a very special birthday gift. Wrapped beautifully in a shoe box were 21 letters Mom had written to me. She had started this tradition the first year of my life and it was her secret until my twenty-first birthday.

BIRTHDAYS

The letters contained memories of the funny things I said and did over the years, the struggles during the teenage situations, times we spent together, differences we had, tears shed, and the love we enjoyed. Thanks, Mom, for the best gift in 21 years.

3

Valentine's Day

This is My commandment, that you love one another, just as I have loved you (John 15:12).

When Observed: February 14
Earliest Observance: Middle Ages

February 14 has become a special day in America, and for one day we turn our hearts to love. I can remember back to my earliest recollection of this special day when I was in elementary school. With great anticipation and thoughtful selection, I chose and signed that special card for that somewhat secret admirer.

Many decades later I still look at February 14 as a special day for expressing love and affection to those special to me. Everyone knows that Valentine's Day is that day of the year when friends and lovers express affection for one another through cards, candy, flowers, or whatever means the imagination can find.

No one is quite certain who this Saint Valentine was. The early lists of church martyrs reveal at least three Valentines, each of whom had his feast day on February 14.

Various legends have come down to us, too. Valentine was said to have been imprisoned and, while there, he cured the jailer's daughter of blindness. Another story, in an attempt to associate him more closely with Valentine's Day, has him falling in love with the jailer's daughter and sending her a letter which he signed, "From Your Valentine."

In the Middle Ages throughout Europe, there was a belief that birds mated on February 14. This belief that birds chose their mates on Valentine's Day led to the idea that boys and girls would do the same. Even at the turn of the twentieth century in the hills of the Ozarks, folks thought that birds and rabbits separately started the mating season on February 14, a day which was for them not only Valentine's Day but Groundhog Day as well.

Some even give credit for this day to the early Roman feast day of Lupercalia, which was celebrated in February in honor of the pastoral god Lupercus, a Roman version of the Greek god, Pan. During this festival the names of young women were put into a box. Youths then drew the names and the boys and girls so matched would be considered partners for the year, which began in March.

The English settlers in the New World brought their Valentine customs with them. Prior to the eighteenth century, original valentine cards of a certain homeliness and simplicity had been exchanged among some of the colonists. But after 1723 the custom really began to grow with the impact from England of valentine writers.

Commercial valentines came out about 1800 and by 1840 were becoming sophisticated. The reduction of postal rates brought about a great increase in the number of valentines sent, and printed valentines became popular. Today, valentine greetings are made to be sent to nearly everyone—friend, relative, and sweetheart alike. Valentine's Day is second only to Christmas in the number of greetings sent in the United States.

Christian Activities

As Christians we can certainly celebrate this holiday with our families and friends better if we can look at the Bible and see how many times love is used to express that feeling and emotion between God and mankind. Our faith is built upon our proper understanding and expression of love. Below are some Scriptures that express God's love to us. May we appreciate our scriptural heritage and through this understanding put into practice to those around us a true expression of love.

Deuteronomy 6:5—"And thou shalt love the Lord thy God

with all thy heart, and with all thy soul, and with all thine might."

Psalm 18:1—"I LOVE Thee, O Lord, my strength."

Psalm 116:1—"I LOVE the Lord, because He hears my voice and my supplications."

Psalm 145:20—"The Lord keeps all who LOVE Him."

Proverbs 8:17—"I LOVE those who LOVE me; and those that seek me will find me."

Romans 8:28—"And we know that God causes all things to work together for good to those who LOVE God. . . ."

Valentine Ideas

On Valentine's Day we have an opportunity to give of ourselves in love. Homemade valentines with lace, ribbon, craft paper, and glue are almost a lost art. Anyone, even the least artistic, can create a lovely valentine, but you can also buy prepackaged valentines.

"Good for" coupons make a great valentine for anyone from

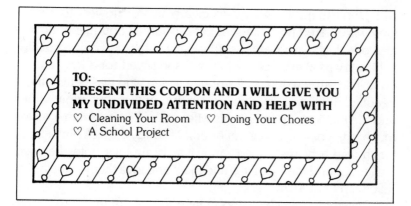

TO: _____
PRESENT THIS COUPON AND I WILL GIVE YOU MY UNDIVIDED ATTENTION AND HELP WITH
♡ Cleaning Your Room   ♡ Doing Your Chores
♡ A School Project

Note: You can photocopy coupons, then color them in.

children to grandparents. They could include:

- one evening of babysitting
- two hours of yard work or weed pulling
- one hour of ironing, sewing, or mending
- cook a meal

Give a gift of your talent as an expression of love. God did in His Son, Jesus; it is the least we can do. What an outreach and even a ministry you can create.

Valentine's Day gives the children an opportunity to give from their hearts. One mother in our neighborhood had Cookie Baking Day with her three girls. They frosted heart-shaped cookies and topped them with jelly beans, coconut, raisins, and nuts and then made up small paper plates filled with loving, homemade cookies and took them to each family on the block. This same idea they carried over to other holidays as well—tree-shaped for Christmas, turkey-shaped for Thanksgiving, cross-shaped for Easter. *What this mother taught her girls was more than making cookies. She taught them to give as Christ gave to us.*

Don't think it's "sissy" to give plants or flowers to a man. One wife shared how she sent her husband a bouquet of flowers at work. He wasn't an executive in a high-rise office building either. It was a sacrifice for her and she saved for a long time to do it. The other workers all stopped to see who was getting those beautiful flowers. They didn't make fun of him, but admired him and the relationship he and his wife had. If flowers seem a bit too much, try a balloon bouquet or box of candy or pack him a fancy lunch with a heart-shaped sandwich. Write love notes between the lettuce and tomato. He'll find them and love them—and hopefully won't eat them.

Valentine's week is a good time to pull out wedding photos and honeymoon pictures. A great way of reminiscing and bringing back special memories.

I save my red leftover Christmas candles for Valentine's week and we have candlelight breakfasts or dinners, children and all.

Red napkins and place mats and white lace doilies make a nice place setting. A paper or fabric heart wreath can be put on your front door or mailbox the week before Valentine's Day. A sure sign of love and welcome to friends, neighbors, and family.

Valentine's Day gives us an excellent opportunity to reach out to others—to send a note, deliver a handmade valentine, or give a basket of homemade goodies.

Perhaps an apology is due to a friend or family member. Now is a perfect time to settle those differences. A note of apology in love could open the doors for good feelings in the future.

Additional Valentine's Ideas

1. Make a large red heart with white lace doilies on the edges and in the middle write the words, "I did it because I love you." Take the card and place it next to something you did to show your love for that person.

- A bed that has been made
- A cleaned sink of dishes
- A cleaned carpet that has been vacuumed

2. Bake a cake and put little notes in it. The children will love it and look forward to it each year. Write some love notes, positive messages, or short Bible verses on strips of paper, fold the papers in small squares, wrap them in foil, and place the notes throughout the cake batter. When the children get a piece of cake they will love to check to see if there's a note in their piece.

3. Plan a dinner by candlelight. Cook a special meal and eat on your good dishes with your prettiest glasses and serving ware in the formal dining room (if you have one). Prepare a special dessert with the children's names on the different pieces or a large cake with a special valentine message. Select for each of the children a special valentine card, even add a few of your own special words. You might even send out a few days ahead of time a special invitation to your dinner party. It is a good opportunity for the family to dress-up special for this candlelight dinner. This

works best when Dad can help in the preparation. Keep the children out of the dining room until they are brought in blindfolded. As they take off the blindfolds, their eyes become large with excitement to see for the first time this special dinner setting. During the meal take turns in expressing how important each member is to the family. Let the children know how special they are to Mom and Dad (by the way, take the phone off the hook).

4. It's easy to make a heart-shaped cake to serve. Just bake a round cake and a square one. Face the square one toward you, point forward like a playing card diamond. Slice the round cake in half and position the two halves against the diamond's uppermost sides. Frost and serve.

5. Give your friends a candy bar "hello." On a piece of posterboard write your valentine greetings so the candy bar forms part of the message. Some suggested messages might include:

- "I [mint] to ask you to be my Valentine."
- "Valentine, you stole a [Big Hunk] of my heart."
- "I chews [gum] you to be my Valentine."
- "You're the [Cup o' Gold] at the end of my rainbow."
- "I'd run a [Marathon Bar] for you, Valentine."

6. When the family comes to breakfast on Valentine's Day morning, have already-prepared pink pancakes. Just add a little food coloring to the batter. The children love it.

7. In preparing sandwiches for the family as they go to school and work, take either a large heart-shaped cookie cutter or with a knife shape your bread into a heart. They will love the surprise when they unwrap the sandwich during the lunch hour.

8. You can make heart-shaped cupcakes easily by using your favorite cupcake recipe. Place paper baking cups in a muffin tin. Put a marble or small ball of foil in each cup, between the paper-liner and pan. This makes a heart-shaped mold in which to cook cupcakes. Pour in batter and bake as usual. Don't fill cups too full or you will lose the heart-shaped effect of the cupcake.

9. Give grandparents a special valentine. Have children decorate a red construction paper heart. Cut out a heart-shape from the middle of the valentine. Glue child's school picture or other recent picture into the heart shape. If the children make one each year, grandparents will have a collection of special valentines to save over the years.

10. Start a week ahead of time and have a valentine card construction party. Gather all the materials and supplies together. Unfold one or two card tables and lay out an old sheet or table-cloth to cover the table surface. Place in an area of the home where the table can be left up for the week. The family can have a fun time constructing their very special valentine cards. A great activity to do before school, after school, in lieu of television or after dinner. Mom and Dad can even get into the swing of things.

11. Husbands and children need to get together and think up something special for Mom. Compose a special card that reflects how you love her. Give her a small, inexpensive gift. Hubby might want to call while at work to whisper a special love message

to that special lady in his life. Send or take home a bouquet of flowers or a potted plant. Wives just love fresh-cut flowers in the home.

12. One mom on Valentine's Day makes a special tea party for her children and their friends. They place at each end of the table Raggedy Ann and Andy. She used her best dishes and cloth napkins. The other moms are invited, but they sit in the kitchen out of the way. It's first-class for the children and a great idea for teens, too!

Easter

4

Easter

He is not here, but He has risen (Luke 24:6).

When Observed: On the Sunday following the first full moon after the vernal equinox, sometime between March 22 and April 25.
Earliest Observance: Second century

Being brought up in the Jewish faith, I had no early experiences with or recollections of Easter in my childhood. I did have a stuffed Easter bunny, colored eggs, a new dress, and new shoes, but I really didn't observe the religious aspects of Easter until I met and married my husband, Bob. At that time I began to realize that Easter had a much more powerful message than what I had experienced.

I became aware that no holy day or festival in the Christian year compares in importance with Easter Sunday. That Jesus Christ was resurrected after having suffered and died is the belief most central to the Christian faith. Christians believe that by His dying, Jesus accomplished a reconciliation between God and man. The apostle Paul says:

> Now if Christ is preached as raised from the dead, how can some of you say that there is no resurrection of the dead? But if there is no resurrection of the dead, then Christ has not been raised; if Christ has not been raised, then our preaching is in vain and your faith is in vain (1 Corinthians 15:12–14).

I also learned in Matthew's gospel that after the crucifixion Joseph of Arimathea placed Jesus in his own tomb and rolled a

39

great stone across the entrance. But the Pharisees and Pilate feared that the disciples might come and steal Jesus' body to fulfill His prophecy, "After three days I will rise again." So the tomb was sealed and a guard was placed around the tomb.

On the third day Mary Magdalene came to the tomb with Mary the mother of James:

> Suddenly there was a great earthquake; for an angel of the Lord came down from heaven and rolled aside the stone and sat on it. His face shone like lightning and his clothing was a brilliant white. The guards shook with fear when they saw Him and fell into a dead faint. Then the angel spoke to the women. "Don't be frightened!" he said. "I know you are looking for Jesus, who was crucified, but He isn't here! For He has come back to life again, just as He said He would. Come in and see where His body was lying. . . . And now, go quickly and tell His disciples that He has risen from the dead, and that He is going to Galilee to meet them there. That is my message to them" (Matthew 28:2–7).

The feast of Easter was well-established by the second century. There was a great deal of controversy over whether the day should be celebrated on a weekday or whether Easter should always be a Sunday regardless of date. In 325 A.D. the Council of Nicaea decided that Easter should fall on the Sunday following the first full moon after the vernal equinox. This calculation was made easier when March 21 was chosen as the date of the vernal equinox.

In the early church, the several days of Pascha commemorated the passion, death, and resurrection of Jesus Christ. By the fourth century, Pascha Sunday had become a separate day which commemorated the glorious resurrection.

In Britain the feast was named Easter after the Anglo-Saxon goddess of spring, Eastre.

Many of the early settlers of America were Puritans or members of Protestant denominations who didn't want anything to do with pagan religious festivals. The celebration of Easter in this country was severely limited. It is well-known that the Puritans in

Massachusetts outlawed the celebration of Christmas and they also tried to play down the observance of Easter as far as possible.

After the Civil War the message and meaning of Easter began to be more widely celebrated when the story of the resurrection was used by the Presbyterians as a logical inspiration of renewed hope for all those bereaved by the war.

Since then the feast has become a major religious and secular celebration. Its joyous customs delight children and adults alike. It is a family day when relatives and friends gather after church services for festive dinners or maybe a park picnic, weather permitting.

Easter heralds the beginning of spring and is generally accompanied by a week's vacation from school.

One of the beautiful religious customs of Easter is the dawn service held by many Christian denominations. These services may well have their origin in the biblical text: "But on the first day of the week, at early dawn, they came to the tomb" (Luke 24:1). The outdoor Easter sunrise service was brought to America by Protestant emigrants from Moravia. The first service was held in Bethlehem, Pennsylvania in 1741.

Many Christians are torn between the religious significance of the biblical account of Christ's life, death, and resurrection and the pagan and secular thrust given to these holidays. We struggle with the concept of being in the world but not of the world. Easter and Christmas seem to have been diluted over the past few decades. We want to honor the Scriptures, but we are also bombarded with the Easter bunny, dyeing eggs, egg hunts, Easter clothing, etc. One of the ways a family might want to separate the secular from the religious is to celebrate Easter Saturday and do all those activities which don't fall into the religious function of the season and which are children's "fun" part of Easter.

Easter Saturday Ideas

1. Decorate and dye your eggs.
2. Hide the eggs in the lawn area of your home or a friend's home, or go to a park and have an Easter egg hunt. You might

even include a "treasure egg" that offers a special prize to the child that discovers it. If your children's ages span several years, you might consider having two separate egg hunts, one for the smaller children and one for the older set.

This hunt can be very involved with the whole family, neighborhood, and friends included or it can be scaled down to include just you and a child. Don't let the lack of numbers discourage you.

3. Inside your "treasure egg" you might want to hide money, a gift, a candy treat, or a small toy.

4. You might want to decorate the serving table in spring colors and serve light refreshments after the hunt.

5. You and your neighbors or friends might want to go in together and hire a local clown or magician to come to the party and entertain the children.

6. There are usually some children who don't find any eggs and others who find more than they can carry. This provides a wonderful opportunity to talk about sharing with others.

7. You might give your children some helpful phrases when decorating their hard-boiled eggs:

He Is Risen	Born Again
Jesus Is Love	For God So Loved the World
Praise God	Jesus Died for You
Jesus Loves You	Lord of Lords

8. You might even want to have an art project in mind to use the eggshells for when they are peeled from the eggs. Since they are colored, cracked, and in small pieces, they make an excellent Easter mosaic. Assemble a large sheet of poster or construction paper, white glue, and assorted colors of broken eggshells. Trace or draw a simple Easter picture onto your piece of paper. Glue the pieces of colored eggshells onto the paper to fill up your drawing.

9. Use a loaf of bread before it is sliced. Cut the top off, leaving the sides and a handle for a basket. Hollow out the bread so Easter goodies can be placed inside and trim with ribbon.

Grind the unused bread for bread crumbs. This becomes an Easter Bread Basket.

10. Personalize your eggs by enclosing Easter messages in the shells. To blow out the raw eggs, use a sharp needle and poke a small hole in the small end of each egg and a larger hole in the big end. Through the larger hole, puncture the egg yolk with the needle. Hold the egg over a bowl and gently blow through the small hole to force the raw egg out of the large hole. Rinse shells carefully and thoroughly.

Decorate blown-out eggshells with marking pens, ribbon, lace, or watercolor paints. Write messages on small pieces of paper. Roll them up and carefully place them inside the eggs through the larger hole. Your messages could contain something related to the Easter story.

Egg Tips:

- If you add two tablespoons vinegar to water before cooking eggs, egg white from cracked eggs will not leak into the water.
- Puncture large end of eggshell with a needle just before cooking to keep eggs from cracking.
- Although fresh eggs can be stored in their cartons in the refrigerator for two to three weeks, hard-cooked eggs should be refrigerated when cooled and used within one week.
- Grate the leftover hard-boiled eggs and place portions in small freezer bags and freeze for later use. Thawed, they provide excellent garnish for green salads. They taste good creamed over toast or added to casseroles. They even make delicious deviled eggs.
- Natural dyes can be put to work at Easter time. You'll have green eggs if you boil them with green grass; red if they're boiled with beets; and yellow if onion skins are in the pot.

11. You and your family might want to make up a special Easter basket for those friends or neighbors who might be in need

of food, clothing, or even a little touch of special loving.

Use Easter Saturday to share the secular activities and reserve Easter Sunday as the day for celebrating and sharing in the death and resurrection of the Lord Jesus Christ.

Easter Sunday Ideas

> And these words, which I am commanding you today, shall be on your heart; and you shall teach them diligently to your sons and shall talk of them when you sit in your house and when you walk by the way and when you lie down and when you rise up (Deuteronomy 6:6,7).

1. Plan with your family to attend an Easter morning sunrise service. Starting the week before as a family, you may want to read a little each day in John 12–20 about the story of the life of Christ leading up to the crucifixion and resurrection. This background will make the sunrise service more meaningful to the children.

2. After a light breakfast, attend a regular church service.

3. Easter is a great time to have the extended family together for lunch or dinner. Rather than one family having full responsibility for food preparation, you might suggest a potluck with various families bringing different parts of the menu. Some families also rotate to a different home each year. This way no one family has the continuous responsibility of hosting the meal year after year.

4. In some large families where the immediate family is not available for celebration at Thanksgiving and/or Christmas, you might use Easter as the holiday when you come together as a total family. You could even use the symbols of Christmas with an Easter flair. Be creative and see how exciting you can make the theme.

5. Around the dining table you could have the Easter story written out and attached to the name tags or napkin rings. Before blessing the food, have various members of the family read their Scripture and share what that verse means to them.

6. Have your children prepare a drama depicting a segment of the Easter story and let the other children or adults try to guess what segment they are portraying.

7. Before the day is over, prepare and share a family communion using bread or crackers and grape juice.

Prepare a loaf of bread (unleavened if possible) and a cup of grape juice so that the family can share taking of the "One Body" and "One Cup" (Read Matthew 26:17–30). If it is your conviction that only a clergyman can administer communion you might invite one of your church's staff members to join you in this part of the celebration.

As you take a piece of the bread you might share with the next person what is so special to you about Easter. Then in a prayer of thanksgiving, express how special Jesus is to you and your family. You might even have several members of the family pray. As the Scriptures state, you can close with a song. (If everyone isn't familiar with the words, you may have printed copies for everyone.)

5

Mother's Day

Honor your father and your mother, that your days may be prolonged in the land which the Lord your God gives you (Exodus 20:12).

When Observed: Second Sunday in May
Earliest Observance in United States: May 10, 1908; Grafton, West Virginia

The first Mother's Day observance was a church service held in Grafton, West Virginia, on May 10, 1908 to honor motherhood and pay homage to Mrs. Anna Reese Jarvis. Her daughter, Anna M. Jarvis, was instrumental in establishing this day to honor mothers in general, but also to honor her own mother.

The carnation which has become so traditional and familiar on Mother's Day was part of this first service. This was one of Mrs. Jarvis' favorite flowers.

By 1911 every state in the Union had adopted its own day for the observance of Mother's Day. On May 9, 1914, a resolution providing that the second Sunday in May be designated Mother's Day was issued by President Woodrow Wilson.

Today Mother's Day is a popular occasion, warm and joyful in spirit. Flowers and gifts are often the order of the day. Greetings are designed to be sent not only to one's own mother but also to grandmothers, aunts, mothers of wives and sweethearts, and to anyone who merits the accolades of motherhood.

When I think of motherhood, I'm reminded of one great mother of the eighteenth century, Sarah Edwards, whose vital interest in her children's development had a lasting impact.

49

Married to the famous clergyman and theologian Jonathan Edwards, she was the mother of 11 children. At the same time, Sarah maintained a vital and intensely loving marriage.

Writing about the Edwards family, author Elizabeth Dodds says straightforwardly, "The way children turn out is always a reflection on their mother."

Dodds refers to a study done by A. E. Winship in 1900 in which he lists some of the accomplishments of the 1,400 Edwards' descendants he located. The Edwards family produced:

13 college presidents
65 professors
100 lawyers and a dean of a law school
30 judges
66 physicians and a dean of a medical school
80 holders of public office
3 United States senators
3 mayors of large cities
3 state governors
1 vice president of the United States
1 controller of the United States Treasury

Winship believed that "much of the capacity and talent, intensity and character of the more than 1,400 of the Edwards family is due to Mrs. Edwards."

How did Sarah Edwards do it? A deeply Christian woman, Sarah emerges from the pages of Dodds' book as a firm, patient mother who treated her children with courtesy and love. Samuel Hopkins, a contemporary who spent time in the Edwards' household, said Sarah was able to guide her children without angry words or blows. Unlike many mothers today, Sarah had only to speak once and her children obeyed her.

"In their manners they were uncommonly respectful to their parents. When their parents came into the room, they all rose instinctively from their seats and never resumed them until their parents were seated."

These children who were so well-treated by their parents in

turn loved and respected them as well as each other.

In the management of her busy colonial home, Sarah puts her modern counterparts to shame. We, who have only to press a button to start our many machines, can hardly imagine the sheer physical labor required of the colonial housewife. Sarah had many hard tasks: to see that the candles and clothes were made, the food prepared, the garden planted, the fire stoked, and the guests fed and comfortably housed. Contiguously, she taught her children to work and deal with life.

Dodds'also portrays Sarah as a keen observer of human nature:

> . . . [she] carefully observed the first appearance of resentment and ill will in her young children, toward any person whatever, and did not connive at it . . . but was careful to show her displeasure and suppress it to the utmost; yet not by angry, wrathful words, which often provoke children to wrath. . . . Her system of discipline was begun at a very early age and it was her rule to resist the first, as well as every subsequent exhibition of temper or disobedience in the child . . . wisely reflecting that until a child will obey his parents, he will never be brought to obey God.

As a disciplinarian, Sarah clearly defined her boundaries and tolerated no misbehavior from her children. The result was a household that emanated love and harmony.

As Elizabeth Dodds makes abundantly clear in her book, a mother is not merely rearing her one generation of children. She is also affecting future generations for good or ill. All the love, nurture, education, and character-building that spring from Mother's work influence those sons and daughters. The results show up in the children's accomplishments, attitudes toward life, and parenting capacity. For example, one of Sarah Edwards' grandsons, Timothy Dwight, president of Yale, (echoing Lincoln) said, "All that I am and all that I shall be, I owe to my mother."

As one ponders this praise, the question arises: Are we women unhappy in our mothering role because we make too little, rather than too much, of that role? Do we see what we have to give our children as minor rather than major, and consequently send them into the world without a healthy core identity and strong spiritual values?

It was the great investment of time that mothers like Sarah Edwards and Susanna Wesley made in the lives of their children that garnered each such high praise. One can't teach a child to read in an hour or stretch a child's mind in a few days.

Have we as mothers unwisely left our children's education to school and church, believing that we can fill in around the edges? And would we feel better about ourselves if we were more actively involved in teaching our children? I think so.

A thread runs throughout the whole of life: Only as we invest much will the yield be great. Our children are growing up in a rough, tough world, and they need us to invest a lot of time and energy in their lives. Only then will they—and we—experience significant gain (Brenda Hunter, "The Value of Motherhood," Focus on the Family, 1986, pp. 9–12).

Wow! What a mother! I could feel real guilty if I compare myself to Sarah Edwards. But I know this, I did the best I knew how to do and so are you. Perfect mom? No, not by a long shot. I learned a lot along the way, and I'm still learning. Being open to God's Word and His promises are all the tools I need to be the mother God is molding me into.

The following acrostic is what MOTHER means to me:

Mother's Daily Prayer to God

Matthew 6:33 says, "Seek ye first the Kingdom of God and His righteousness and all these things shall be added unto you." This verse establishes my first priority. I set aside time each day for prayer.

The "prayer basket" I made up for myself contains my Bible, pen, a box of tissue, stationery, a few silk flowers in a small jar, and my prayer notebook.

My prayer notebook is a three-ring binder with prayer request sheets, tabs labeled Monday through Sunday and sheets for sermon notes.

I organized this to give me "More Hours In My Day" yet

spending quality time with my Lord and praying for all the needs of my family and friends.

For each day of the week I've delegated several topics to pray for. Example: Monday—home organization; family. I have a page for each immediate member of the family—Bob, Brad, Craig, Jenny, etc. For each grandchild I've placed their hand print on their page and drawn a heart in the middle. On Monday when I pray for them, I place my hand on theirs and our hearts beat together as I give the Lord my requests. Tuesday—illnesses; my Auntie Phyllis who broke her hip; Brooke, who has M.S. Wednesday—our church pastor and staff people. Thursday—self, personal finances. Friday— our country, city, state, President. Saturday—Missionaries at home and abroad. Sunday—sermon notes; this is where I record

and outline the sermon, any church prayer requests. Later, these requests can be filtered into the proper tab section. Scriptures can be recorded for future references.

My prayer basket goes with me wherever I spend time in prayer. Perhaps it's the backyard under a tree in the summer; by a lake or a stream; by the fireplace in the winter with a cup of tea; in an office, bedroom, or perhaps in the bathroom where I know I can be alone. My prayer basket has all the tools I need to "seek first the kingdom of God."

*O*pen to Him

I want to have a heart like Jesus. Psalm 139 says it all:

Lord, you have examined me and you know me. You know everything I do; from far away you understand all my thoughts. You see me, whether I am working or resting; you know all my actions. Even before I speak, you already know what I will say. You are all around me on every side; you protect me with your power. Your knowledge of me is too deep; it is beyond my understanding . . . You created every part of me; you put me together in my mother's womb. I praise you because you are to be feared; all you do is strange and wonderful. I know it with all my heart. When my bones were being formed, carefully put together in my mother's womb, when I was growing there in secret, you knew that I was there—you saw me before I was born. The days allotted to me had all been recorded in your book, before any of them ever began . . . Examine me, O God and know my mind; test me, and discover my thoughts. Find out if there be any evil in me and guide me in the everlasting way" (TEV).

*T*rust Him

In all things mold us in the Word. Our hope as a mom is found in time with our Bibles to study His Word.

*H*ealing Through Him

Relationships are forgiven so that a healing process can take place. If mother and daughter or mother and son have out-of-order relationships, these must be brought to the surface and bathed with prayer for a complete cleansing.

When my mother went home to be with the Lord at 78 years of age, she left me with two very beautiful gifts: her belief in the Messiah and that one day we will be in Glory together, and the memory of all the loving times of sweet fellowship we had together.

Guilt feelings can eat you up inside—so clean out the wounds and pour the healing ointment of love inside.

*E*nriched by Him

Teach us, O Lord, so we can teach others. Titus 2:4 says that the older women are to teach the younger women to love their husbands and to be makers of a home. That's what Sarah Edwards did as a mother. We can take our life's experiences and teach them to others and through it all you, too, will learn.

*R*each up to Him

I'm choosing to make God the Lord of my life. This is the best choice I can make; it gives me a purpose and a peace during the earthquake times.

Let's exchange our earthly desires for heavenly desires. We'll be more alive in death than in life when we do, and our beautiful years of motherhood will never end. Our hearts can daily reach up to God in love and prayer.

I received this letter from our son, Brad, one year on Mother's Day when he was away at college. It was the best gift I've ever received from him and yet it cost only his time.

Thank You, God,

For pretending not to notice that one of Your angels is missing and for guiding her to me. You must have known how much I would need her, so You turned Your head for a minute and allowed her to slip away to me. Sometimes I wonder what special name You had for her. I call her "Mother." To think of not having her with me is unbearable. I don't know what I would have done without her all these years. She has loved me without reservation—whether I deserved to be loved or not. Willingly and happily, she has fed me, clothed me, taught me, encouraged me, inspired me, and with her own special brand of gentleness reprimanded me. A bit of heaven's own blue, her eyes reflect hope and love for You and her family. She has tried to instill that love in us. She's not the least bit afraid of work. With her constant scrubbing, polishing, painting, and fixing she has made every house we've lived in, a beautiful home. When I'm confused, she sets me straight. She knows what matters and what doesn't. What to hold on to and what to let go. You have given her an endless supply of love. She gives it away freely yet never seems to run low. Even before I am aware I have a need, she is making plans and working to supply it. You gave her great patience. She is the best listener I have met. With understanding and determination she always seems to turn a calamity into some kind of success. She urges me to carry my own load in life but is always close by if I stumble under the burden. She hurts when I hurt. She cries when I cry. And she will not be happy until she has seen a smile on my face once more. Although she has taught me to pray, she has never ceased to invoke Your richest blessings upon me. Thank the other angels for filling in for her while she is away. I know it hasn't been easy. Her shoes would be hard to fill. She has to be one of Your greatest miracles, God, and I want to thank you for lending my Mother to me."

Special Gifts

Gifts of yourself may be the greatest gift Mom will ever receive. Here are a few ideas:

1. *The gift of a compliment*—Perhaps you could make a list of the qualities you admire in your mother: her sense of humor, her survival instinct, her ability to live without impossible expectations. You might praise her cooking, her patience, her intelligence, or her sensitivity.

2. *A gift of thanks*—It's strange how much we take from others and how little we return. A thank-you is a simple act, not always expected and therefore very valuable. A thanks for having endured the years of childhood that required her constant atten-

tion. The thousands of meals she cooked. The tons of laundry she did. And most important, for just being there.

3. *A gift of affection*—How about a warm embrace, a kiss on the cheek, a moment of hand-holding? All of us need affection no matter what our age or how much we protest that it's not our style.

4. *A gift of listening*—Everyone has known the frustration of wanting to be heard and finding that no one is interested in listening. One of the most valuable things we can do for each other is to be a good listener.

5. *The gift of a note*—You might write your mother a personal note, unabashedly sentimental, full of loving thoughts—which may become her newest family treasure. If you find yourself lacking the right words, a simple "Mom, I love you" can say so much.

6. *A gift of forgiveness*—People are not perfect. Those closest to us often seem the least so. We owe them the same forgiveness we expect for our own imperfections. An act of forgiveness can start things anew and reunite us as nothing else can.

If none of these gifts satisfy you, try a gift of laughter. Nothing unites like laughter. Perhaps you can take her out for a day of doing all the crazy things she used to love. Just a day for accumulating new, joyous memories between mother and daughter or son.

Gifts of Self

None of these gift suggestions cost anything, yet each is one of a kind and bound to please because it's a gift of yourself.

Every day should be a day in which we honor all members of our family, but this day should be special just for Mom.

1. If you still live at home with Mom, get with Dad and plan some special activities for her. Really make a big deal out of this day.

- Treat Mom with breakfast in bed.
- A delightful gift if you are low on money is to give Mom a cute coupon stating that it is good for:

    clearing off the dinner dishes for a week
    doing the ironing for a week
    loading the dishwasher (or washing by hand) for a
    week.

- You might want to plan a picnic for Mom.
- Use an oven mitt as the wrapping for a small gift.
- Take Mom to church and share with her how you appreciate her giving you a Christian training, a big thank-you for the prayers she shares with you each night, etc. After church you can go out for brunch (if you do, be sure to make reservations at least two weeks in advance) or prepare a brunch for her at home. Mom will love the special treatment.

2. If you no longer live at home, you still need to take time to honor Mom.

- Take or send her flowers.
- Take or send her a card.
- If out-of-town, start early and give her a telephone call (since the telephone lines are extremely busy on Mother's Day, you might even try to make that call the day before).
- If you are close enough to see her on this day, set up a time to be with her.

Take this opportunity to make Mom feel very special on this, her day.

Father's
Day

6

Father's Day

Grandchildren are the crown of old men, and the glory of sons is their fathers (Proverbs 17:6)

When observed: Third Sunday in June
Earliest Observance: July 5, 1908; Fairmont, West Virginia

Father's day is a relatively new holiday in America. It is a day set aside to honor our living fathers; however, many people do use this day to remember those fathers who have died. Instilling both Mother's Day and Father's Day traditions in youngsters is often the role of the "other" parent. Even though the honoree is not *your* parent, children first need to see an example of loving-kindness toward parents in order to imitate it.

A number of persons have unconnectedly figured in the growth of Father's Day. The earliest mention we have of a day for fathers is July 5, 1908, when a Father's Day service was held in the Central Church of Fairmont, West Virginia, by Dr. Robert T. Webb at the request of Charles Clayton.

In 1912 at the suggestion of the Reverend J. H. Berringer, pastor of the Irvington Methodist Church, the people of Vancouver, Washington conducted a celebration. They believed it to be the first such ceremony.

Another important figure in the "honor fathers" movement was Harry C. Meek, past president of the Uptown Lions Club of Chicago who said that he first had the idea for Father's Day in 1915. He began to suggest it in speeches before various Lions Clubs, and the notion took hold. Members set the date for Father's Day on the third Sunday in June, the Sunday nearest

Meek's birthday. The Lions crowned him "Originator of Father's Day."

Father's Day's most influential promoter was Mrs. John Bruce Dodd of Spokane, Washington. Her father, William Jackson Smart, had accomplished the amazing task of raising six children after his wife died at an early age. She wanted to honor him for this unselfish feat.

President Calvin Coolidge recommended the national observance of this day in 1924, though President Woodrow Wilson had officially approved the idea as early as 1916.

The rose is the official Father's Day flower—a white rose for remembrance, and a red rose as a tribute to a living father.

In 1972 the day finally was established permanently when President Richard Nixon signed a Congressional resolution. His action eliminated the need for an annual designation and put Father's Day on the same continuing basis as Mother's Day. Giving gifts has become a natural part of the occasion, and greetings for fathers, grandfathers, uncles, brothers, sons, other relatives, and friends are widely sent. Father's Day has become another happy occasion for family dinners and gatherings. This day is an occasion to establish more intimate relations between fathers and their children, and to impress upon fathers the full measure of their responsibilities and obligations.

Spiritual Teachings

Fathers play such a large part in developing the authority awareness of God. Children learn this by watching their father's everyday words and actions. I have always tried to model in front (and behind) our children the respect that we give fatherhood. Some of those traits are: love, respect, submission, godliness, speaking at all times with admiration, honoring his position of leadership, and respecting his decision-making responsibilities.

Exodus 20:12 states, "Honor your father and your mother. . . ." I've attempted to teach my children at home to give proper honor to their father. We have honored him through: obeying him in his position of authority; being careful of the language used in the home; and by showing kindness, politeness, discipline, etc. As our children have grown older they are more in love with their father than ever before. Not because he is always right or sinless, but because the children receive blessings by honoring their father. This is not easy at all times, because obedience often isn't easy! We make a deliberate choice to honor our fathers. As mothers we can be of great help to our children and family in helping develop the harmony that is necessary to build a warm and loving family.

I have learned over the years to make every day of the year Father's Day. Fathers play such a large part in making a family successful in the sight of God. Except for God Himself, our next priority is the father of our home. We need to make a deliberate effort each day to find time for the men of our homes. If we don't have a husband or father at home because of some circumstance, we might want to adopt another man to help out in these times. If the children's real father is alive we need to encourage them to take time on this day to say "I love you."

Ideas

1. *Designer Dad*—A crayon drawing of Dad translates into an exclusive, designer T-shirt. The artist should use dark colors and a heavy hand with the crayons on a separate piece of paper. DAD must be written backwards (ᗡAᗡ) to appear correctly on the shirt. Place the crayon drawing on a white T-shirt and iron at cotton temperature. T-shirt shops have transfers on every subject.

2. *Cards*—Help the children design and make their own Father's Day cards. Dads love homemade cards with selected verses handwritten. They all say "I love you."

3. *Just Daddy and Me*—At church you might want to plan a brunch just for the fathers and their daughters. Have each share introductions, good food (physical as well as spiritual), and a fun time with each other. It is their special date on this special day.

4. *Kidnap Dad*—Create a plan for kidnapping your dad from work to have lunch together. (You might need some help from Mom to pull this off.)

5. *Popcorn Pop*—Fix and eat together a bowl of popcorn. (Try it without TV—try conversation instead.)

6. *Write a Note*—Write a brief thank-you note to Dad stating your appreciation and encouragement for all he does for you and the family. Last year our son, Brad, wrote his dad this special letter for Father's Day. Needless to say, it had a real impact on Bob's life. It certainly drew the two closer together because Brad took time to say, "Thanks, Dad."

Dear Dad:

I have a moment and thought I would drop a line. . . .

As I go through this important time in my life, I really begin to realize what I have in front of me. It's not going to be easy. However, because of all the time you put into my life, it is going to be a lot easier tackling the "real world." I feel like I know the value of money and what it means to earn it. (And save it, too!)

As I look back on my college career I realize how fortunate I am that I had such an understanding dad that was flexible with me. Most of all I want you to know that I appreciate your financial support over the past 5 years. That shows me that you are a very giving father and I hope someday to be as giving as you have been to me.

I have gone through a lot of stages in my life and I think I am slowly ending another one. I have really been getting into my job and spending a lot of time with it. I am slowly phasing away from the fraternity. It's hard to do but I think it is very good for me to move on. It's going to be very hard for me to leave some of my best friends that mean so much to me.

Dad, I just want to thank you for all the time you have spent pruning me to become the man, husband, and father I will someday be. Your time spent with me as a young boy was very effective in determining the type of gentleman I am and will be. Thank you for every single thing you have done and encouraged me to do. I respect you very much (as do my friends) and I hope I can contribute as much as you have to this world someday. I Love You!!

Love, Your son
Brad

I Love You too, Mom!! OXOXOXOXOX

7. *Gift Subscription*—Give your dad a year's subscription to *Dads Only*, P.O. Box 340, Julian, CA 92036. An excellent Christian-based magazine for dads. It gives practical ideas on how to be a better dad.

8. *The Gift of a Compliment*—Perhaps you could make a list of the qualities you admire in your father: his sense of humor; his survival instinct; his ability to live without impossible expectations; his provision for the family; his godly attributes; his warmth, affection, kindness, and unselfishness.

9. *A Gift of Affection*—How about a warm embrace, a kiss on the cheeks, a moment to hold his hand? All of us need affection no matter what our age or how much we protest that it's not our style.

10. *A Gift of Forgiveness*—People are not perfect. Those closest to us often seen the least so. We owe them the same forgiveness we expect for our own imperfections. An act of forgiveness can start things anew and reunite us as nothing else can.

11. *Gifts of Self*—None of these gift suggestions costs anything, yet each is one-of-a-kind and bound to please because it's a gift of yourself. Every day should be a day in which we honor all members of our family, but this day should be special just for Father.

—If you live at home with Dad, get with Mom and plan some special activities for him. Really make a big deal out of this day.
- Treat Dad with breakfast in bed.
- A delightful gift if you are low on money is to give Dad a cute coupon stating that it is good for:
  One free washing of the family car
  One free back rub
  One shoeshine
  Free time to read the newspaper
  with no interruptions
- Plan a picnic for Dad.
- Take Dad out to brunch after church (be sure to make reservations first).
- Dad doesn't have to do any work on this special day.

— If you no longer live at home, you still need to take time to honor Dad.

- Send him a hanging plant for the patio, or a plant for his office.
- Give him a telephone call. (Since the telephone lines are extremely busy on Father's Day, you might even try to make the call the day before.)
- Send two tickets for a sporting event, musical concert, or some other activity he would enjoy.

12. *Read Proverbs to Me*—If you are a teenage boy ask your father to read the Book of Proverbs to you. There are 31 chapters and you can read one each day. My Bob did this for our son when he was 15 and it provides a great time together for father and his son(s) (daughters can also be included).

13. *Gifts of Special Tools*—Many times Dad is in special need of some tools for his garage or automobile. Remember those special times when he has said, "I sure wish I had _____, it would make my job so much easier." Those are cue words for the future gift list. Dads are practical in nature and really appreciate practical gifts.

Take this opportunity to make Father feel very special on this, his day.

Last year in our local newspaper there appeared a reprint from a previous Ann Landers article dealing with Father's Day; it originally appeared in the Danbury (Connecticut) *News-Times*. I thought it had great wisdom for all of us on this celebration.

FATHER

4 Years: My Daddy can do anything

7 Years: My Dad knows a lot, a whole lot.

8 Years: My Father doesn't know quite everything.

12 Years: Oh, well, naturally Father doesn't know that either.

14 Years: Father? Hopelessly old-fashioned.

21 Years: Oh, that man is out of date. What did you expect?

25 Years: He knows a little bit about it, but not much.

30 Years: Maybe we ought to find out what Dad thinks.

35 Years: A little patience. Let's get Dad's assessment before we do anything.

50 Years: I wonder what Dad would have thought about that. He was pretty smart.

60 Years: My Dad knew absolutely everything!

65 Years: I'd give anything if Dad were here so I could talk this over with him. I really miss that man.

7

Independence Day

And you shall know the truth, and the truth shall make
you free (John 8:32).

When Celebrated: Fourth of July
First Celebration: 1776

This is our grand national holiday—the glorious fourth; when all Americans manifest their patriotic enthusiasm in various ways.

The military marks the day by firing a salute of 13 guns and reading the Declaration of Independence. All over the country, church bells are rung in memory of the Liberty Bell that proclaimed independence. This most famous bell was actually made in England and around its rim are these prophetic words:

"Proclaim liberty throughout the land unto all the inhabitants thereof."

The earliest celebration in 1776 was a very exciting and cheerful occasion. At last the colonies were independent from England. There was yelling and screaming, bonfires were lit, and people paraded and danced in the streets.

The Fourth of July is still celebrated in much the same fashion; there are parades, dancing, and fireworks (some communities are placing certain restrictions due to possible fire dangers).

Since the Fourth of July falls in the summertime and the children are out of school, parents can take their families on outings to the park, in the country, or at the seashore.

This holiday commemorates the formal adoption of the

71

Declaration of Independence by the Continental Congress in Philadelphia on July 4, 1776. Although the resolution for independence was passed by Congress on July 2 and most of the members did not sign the declaration until August 2, the Fourth of July has always been celebrated as the anniversary of national independence. The president of the Congress, John Hancock, did make it official with his signature on that date.

As you and your families celebrate this day, you can elect to be an originator of traditions in your family or you may elect to join in other people's traditions. Either way it is a wonderful time of the year. Several ideas follow that might help you do something different this year.

1. *Backyard barbecue*—The theme of decorations is so easy: red, white, and blue. All the way from the invitations to the napkins you can carry through the patriotic colors of our flag. Be sure to plan at least four weeks ahead with your invitations. People make plans early and need to make decisions regarding what they are going to do. Use the family for suggestions on what the menu will be, what games will be played, and who is going to be on the guest list. The backyard barbecue can branch out to a park setting if it gets too big. Big is fun on this kind of celebration.

2. *Games*—All kinds of games can be explored for this day. Ask the grandparents what kind of games they or their parents use to play when they were young. These older and often forgotten games are a delight. One such old game is called "pickup sticks" or "Jack Straws." Cut any number of sticks of wood $\frac{1}{2}'' \times \frac{1}{2}'' \times 14''$ and paint them three different colors—red, white, and blue. Throw them in a basket or drop them on the ground in a pile. Ask the children to remove one at a time without moving the other sticks. You can make up rules depending on the age of the children and have colorful prizes for the winners.

A very simple contest that requires only a baseball for equipment is to draw a circle three feet in diameter on the ground and see if anyone can stand at the edge, throw the ball straight up into the air and have it land back in the circle.

3. *Sack races*—Go to your local grain store and purchase several grain sacks depending upon the size of your group. Lay

72

out a course that has a start and finish line. The length of the course can vary depending on the age of the participants.

4. *Three-legged race*—This is a similar activity. However, instead of using a grain bag, you tie one leg each of two people together. They line up behind the starting line and at "go" they hop their way to the finish line.

5. *Pop bottle fill*—You'll need pop bottles of the same size, a large bucket of water, and paper cups. Place the large bucket of water in the center of a circle of adults who are laying on their backs on the grass with their feet pointing away from the bucket of water and their heads about six feet from the water bucket. The adults, while lying down, place a pop bottle on their forehead. The children are given paper cups. The object is to have the children run to the bucket of water at "go", fill their cups with water, hurry to their parent's pop bottle, and try to empty their cups into the bottle. As you can imagine, the adults will get soaked. Of course, the prize goes to the team that fills the pop bottle first.

6. *Egg toss*—This activity carries the anticipation that the next toss will cover someone with egg. You play with a partner. Have the partners line up facing each other (the distance apart depends upon the age of the group. Young children will stand close to start out and older children might be six to ten feet apart. Give each team one raw egg in the shell. At the starters command, the person holding the egg will toss the egg in an underhand motion to his partner. If the egg breaks, the team is eliminated from the game. If not, the partners stay in the game. (If the egg hits the ground but doesn't break, the partners stay in the game.) The starter will give directions for those remaining to step back one giant step. Again the person makes an underhand toss of the egg. Those who have eggs intact will continue playing the game until one set of partners is left in the game with a good egg. You might want to suggest that contestants remove their rings, and be sure to have some hand towels to clean up any messy egg splashes. You can also substitute water balloons for the eggs.

7. *Running events*—These are always great fun for the children. They love to try to win. Be sure to divide the children into

age groups so the competition will be fair.

8. *Wheelbarrow races*—Be sure not to have the races too long because young children don't have strong arm muscles. This game is played as a team. One partner holds the other by the ankles and follows behind him to the finish line. You might even want to have the partners reverse positions and come back to the starting line. A fun game!

Remember to have plenty of inexpensive prizes available for the winners. Be sure that all children get participant prizes. It's important that everyone leaves the day feeling that he or she was a winner.

9. *Parade*—Have a family parade—the children love it. Get pots and pans, tambourines, horns, and toy instruments. Small children can carry a flag or tie colored balloons onto strollers, wagons, and tricycles. Everyone can march around the neighborhood and ask others to join in the parade. For country folks, a hayride would be great fun or decorate horses and have a parade. This is a time when small communities can rally together and have fun. A nice ending to the parade would be an ice cream social or a hot dog roast.

Decorating

You can buy red-and-white potted flowers like chrysanthemums, put them in a basket, and place moss or strawlike material around them. Tie a blue bow on the top or place flags around the basket. You can use red, white, and blue streamers down the table.

We have a welcome duck outside our front door. I dress him up depending on the holiday. So he could wear a red, white, and blue ribbon around his neck or a scarf around his head.

If you are having a barbecue, ask your guests to come dressed in red, white, and blue. Make name tags in the shape of a flag using red, white, and blue construction paper. Be sure to put out the American flag. It is an honor to be an American.

Thanksgiving

8

Thanksgiving

Always giving thanks for all things in the name of our Lord Jesus Christ . . . (Ephesians 5:20).

When Observed: Fourth Thursday in November
Earliest Observance: 1621 in Plymouth, Massachusetts

The Pilgrims, who in 1621 observed our first Thanksgiving holiday in Plymouth, Massachusetts, were thankful for their harvest in the New World. They had suffered a perilous journey on the Mayflower, a dreadfully cold first winter, and a large number of deaths. By most standards, the first harvest was very mediocre. Many of the first crops were failures. This first Thanksgiving lasted for three days and was celebrated with enthusiasm. The menu was extensive and the food abundant. The Indian braves had added five deer to the store of meat. They had venison, duck, goose, seafood, eels, white bread, cornbread, leeks, watercress, and a variety of greens. Wild plums and dried berries were served for dessert.

Although turkeys were plentiful, there is no record that they were eaten on this first Thanksgiving holiday.

Records of following Thanksgiving celebrations are rather sporadic. Many of the later colonies did not adopt this harvest celebration. The first national Thanksgiving proclamation was issued by George Washington in 1789. Mrs. Sarah Josepha Hale of Boston had a great deal of influence on the government to have this day celebrated across the nation. In 1863 President Abraham Lincoln made a Thanksgiving Day proclamation to establish this as a national holiday of thanksgiving to be observed on the last Thursday of November. In 1941 Congress changed the day to be the fourth Thursday in November.

For the last 100 years in America, we have begun to develop some meaningful traditions to make this one of the most memorable of all our holidays.

Thanksgiving is warm hearts, good food, family, and lots of conversation. However, some people don't have these kinds of memories.

I was talking with a woman at one of my seminars who had memories of absolutely nothing. Thanksgiving wasn't different from any other day. Today she creates memories, making them happen on purpose. "We talk about what we can do for others weeks before Thanksgiving," she said. "The children become a part of special giving times."

One Thanksgiving a family went to skid row in downtown Los Angeles and helped serve Thanksgiving dinner. They'll never forget that day. It was such a joy that the children suggested they do it again for Christmas.

One year Bob and I were doing a Holiday Seminar at a very alive church in the heart of a low economic area in El Monte, California. It was November 20 and the church was full. The ladies of the church were in a back room busily pulling food from shopping bags. We were so busy ourselves setting up tables and seminar props that we didn't really take notice of exactly what they were doing.

After the first half of my presentation and the refreshments, they did a wonderful thing. Women came from that back room carrying the most beautiful Thanksgiving "love baskets" filled with the complete ingredients for a Thanksgiving dinner from fruit to turkey and pumpkin pies, 32 baskets in all. They then proceeded to hand them out to each single person there.

As I watched those people come forward to receive their baskets, I saw eyes filled with tears: single working parents, single college students, some obviously who didn't have finances for such a meal. That church wanted to give and create a memory, and they sure did. Among the group was a young man who played the piano that day for the singing time. His wife had left him with three young children and he was currently unemployed and living in a small rented apartment. When he went forward to receive his basket, he sobbed with joy. Bob and I were touched by the beauty of that day. We had so much and had taken so much for granted.

If you don't know of a needy family, find one. Call the Salvation Army in your area and ask them how to get in touch with a needy family. Then decide ways you can help make a special memory for them this holiday.

Since Thanksgiving preparation can take up such a large part of November, you might want to use one of our calendar pages found in Exhibit D, and jot down what needs to be done in little bits and pieces to make this a manageable time rather than a stressful one. Starting with the first week in November, delegate each day to accomplish some of these activities.

First Week in November

As we approach the first week in November, we can begin our holiday organization. Creating memories takes time, and organization for the holidays will give us the time we need.

To polish your silver, add one teaspoon of ammonia to your silver polish. You'll get a super shine, plus it prolongs the shine well into the next year. So do it early and enjoy beautiful silver for the holidays.

Toothpaste on a damp cloth is also a good silver polish for that last-minute spoon you forgot that you want to put in the cranberry sauce dish.

Early in the month invite your guests for Thanksgiving dinner. A cheery phone invitation or a written invitation is always welcome.

November: Week 1—Things to Do

Activity	Done (x)
1. _____	☐
2. _____	☐

3. _____ ☐
4. _____ ☐
5. _____ ☐
6. _____ ☐
7. _____ ☐
8. _____ ☐
9. _____ ☐
10. _____ ☐

Second Week in November

Make up your Thanksgiving dinner menu and at the same time compile your marketing list. The days before Thanksgiving you can pick up the dry goods and staples for your meal like stuffing mix, cranberry sauce, applesauce, water chestnuts, etc. It's easier on the budget and makes shopping faster. Check off items on your marketing list as you purchase them. Don't forget the parsley for garnishes. Parsley stays super fresh for weeks if rinsed well and wrapped in a paper towel. Put it into a plastic storage bag, pressing the air out and sealing it tightly.

Plan your Thanksgiving table setting and centerpiece early. Check your silver pieces, plates, and serving dishes to be sure you have enough for the amount of guests you are inviting.

Table decorations can be easy and creative. Take large apples and core out enough to hold a votive candle. Squeeze lemon juice around the cutout area and then place in the candle. These can be set in front of each person's place or down the center of the table with autumn leaves, pods, grapes, pears, corn, eggplant, and even squash and nuts. When the candles are lit, you'll have a beautiful harvest display. Plus you can use the makings of a centerpiece after Thanksgiving for a fruit salad or soup.

If you don't have votive candles, use tall tapers or whatever you have available. This idea can also be used for Christmas with red and green apples.

Here's an activity with a purpose: Take the children or grandchildren on a harvest walk and collect fall leaves of all sizes. Talk about the different colors and shapes of the leaves. Also collect pods that have fallen from the trees. Carefully put them in a bag or basket and bring them home. The leaves can be dipped in melted paraffin and laid out on wax paper and then used for your harvest table decorations. The pods and small leaves along with nuts, plastic grapes, small silk flowers, and even an artificial bird can be used in making a hat for your pumpkin. Just take a whole pumpkin—find one that is sort of fat and squatty—but do not cut into it. With a hot glue gun, glue on the top of the pumpkin a nesting type material like gray moss or sphagnum moss. On top of that, glue the small leaves, nuts, flowers, a bow, or silk flowers. This can be used as a centerpiece with fruits and nuts around it, candles in the apples, figurines of pilgrims, etc.

You and the family will be so proud of this masterpiece, and it will last for several weeks. When Thanksgiving is over simply pry off the hat and store it away until next year to put on top of a new pumpkin.

Name cards can be done ahead of time. Every year, we as a family find verses with a thankful theme. Take a 3×5 card and fold it in half and stand it up on the table. On the front write the name of the person who will sit at that place and inside write the thankful Scripture. When everyone is seated each person then reads his verse and that can be the table blessing.

Another idea is to place at each person's seat a 3×5 card and pen and have each person write something for which they are thankful. These can be read during, before, or after the meal.

On another 3×5 card have each person write one positive quality about someone else. Examples: "I love you, Uncle Brad because you make me laugh with your cute jokes" or "I love you Auntie Christy because you read to me."

This will give a great opportunity to show God's love and the Scriptures will put God's Word into the hearts of those who are not in tune with the Lord. The Bible says, "His Word will not return void." For 32 years we've been feeding God's Word into my Jewish family through the name cards.

At first they were embarrassed to read them and felt a bit timid so we would skip those who didn't feel comfortable. But today, 32 years later, they are the ones who ask to read first. I'm excited because I know 32 verses of God's loving Word have entered their hearts. His Word is sharper than any two-edged sword and we're trusting God to pierce their hearts with His love. A silent witness can be given in so many ways—especially during the harvest season and Thanksgiving Day when people are open to talking about being thankful.

November: Week 2—Things to Do

	Activity	Done (x)
1.		☐
2.		☐
3.		☐
4.		☐
5.		☐
6.		☐
7.		☐
8.		☐
9.		☐
10.		☐

Third Week in November

Make any last minute arrangements for Thanksgiving. If you'll be going out-of-town, ask a neighbor to collect your mail and newspapers. If you are cooking, finalize your menu and entertainment plans.

November: Week 3—Things to Do

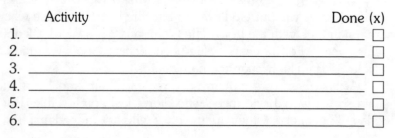

	Activity	Done (x)
1.		☐
2.		☐
3.		☐
4.		☐
5.		☐
6.		☐

7. _____ ☐
8. _____ ☐
9. _____ ☐
10. _____ ☐

Fourth Week in November

I get so excited by this time and thankful for all I have done and already accomplished toward being ready for Thanksgiving.

Special holiday events will be happening Thanksgiving weekend. Decide which event you want to attend as a family, then schedule one special event for each child individually.

A few days before any holiday meal, I plan and organize my serving dishes. Then I make out 3×5 cards, listing on each card what will go into the empty dish, and I place that card in the bowl. That way I don't have to try to remember at the last minute what goes into what. It also makes it easy for guests to help with final preparations.

As you gather around the bountiful table, holding hands can make this a special family and friendship time. Colossians 1:3 says, "We give thanks to God, the Father of our Lord Jesus Christ. . . ." Have a beautiful turkey day filled with thanksgiving to God and don't forget to serve the cranberry sauce or garnish the platter with parsley.

Now put away the fall decorations and start thinking toward Christmas.

November: Week 4—Things to Do

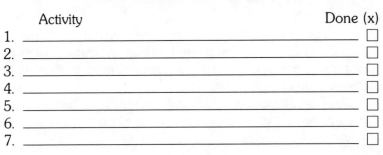

Activity   Done (x)
1. _____ ☐
2. _____ ☐
3. _____ ☐
4. _____ ☐
5. _____ ☐
6. _____ ☐
7. _____ ☐

8. _____ ☐
9. _____ ☐
10. _____ ☐

Some Extra Thanksgiving Ideas

How to Decide How Much Turkey to Buy

For turkeys 12 pounds or smaller, allow about one pound per person. Larger birds have a higher proportion of meat to bone weight. For a 12- to 24-pound turkey, allow about ¾ pound per person. If you want leftovers, allow two pounds per person when buying a turkey 12 pounds or smaller. Allow 1½ pounds per person for 12- to 24-pound birds.

Turkey Tips

1. To store a fresh turkey, loosely cover it with waxed paper or foil. Keep in the coldest part of your refrigerator and cook within three days.

2. You can special order your turkey from your favorite market. Give them the weight you want and request that it be fresh, not frozen. Pick it up the day before Thanksgiving. You now have a fresh turkey that is ready for the oven.

3. After cooking the turkey, it may be stored three or four days in the refrigerator or frozen and stored up to three months.

4. Keep a frozen turkey in the freezer until you want to cook it. Whole turkeys can be kept frozen for one year, turkey parts for six months.

5. Thaw your frozen turkey in the refrigerator or place in cold water or leave at room temperature. Keep the plastic wrapper on the turkey. For even thawing at room temperature, place the wrapped turkey in a brown paper bag.

6. The refrigerator is the best place to thaw your turkey. It keeps meat cold while it defrosts. Allow five hours per pound to thaw.

Roasting Time for Turkeys

Size	Stuffed	Unstuffed
8–12 lbs.	4–5 hours	3–4 hours
12–16 lbs.	4½–6 hours	3½–5 hours
16–20 lbs.	5½–7 hours	4½–6 hours
20–24 lbs.	6½–7½ hours	5½–6½ hours

Oven temperature 325°F (165°C)

The meat thermometer should register 185°F (85°C) in the thickest part of the thigh when done. Juices should run clear when the bird is pierced with a fork between the leg and thigh.

These times are guidelines only.

Steps to Standard Turkey Cooking (Option #1)

1. Wash the turkey well and wipe dry with paper towels. Season the cavity of the bird.
2. Stuff with a favorite dressing.
3. Rub olive oil or Crisco all over the turkey.
4. Use a meat thermometer if possible, placing it in the thickest part of the thigh and being careful not to hit a bone.
5. Sprinkle with salt and pepper.
6. Place the turkey on a rack in a roasting pan with breast up (however, breast down makes a turkey moist).
7. Place aluminum foil over the turkey and pan with the thermometer sticking out for ease in reading.
8. Place turkey and pan in the oven set at 325°F (165°C).
9. Remove the foil from the turkey the last 30 minutes for final browning.
10. Use the juices to pour over the bird to assist in the browning process. Be very careful that you don't burn yourself when basting the bird.
11. Let the turkey cool at least 30–60 minutes before carving.

Perfect Every Time Turkey (Option #2)

Trust me with this one. I've been making at least four turkeys a year for 32 years and this recipe from Adelle Davis is the best of any I've ever done. The white meat will melt in your mouth.

I have always used a meat thermometer so even with this method I still do—just so I know for sure when it's done.

This is a slow roasting method, but once in the oven you can forget it until it comes out.

Choose desired size turkey, wash it well, and remove the neck and giblets. Dry turkey with paper towels, salt the cavity, and stuff with brown rice dressing or dressing of your choice. Rub the outside well with pure olive oil.

Put the turkey breast down (this bastes itself, making white meat very moist) on a poultry rack in a roasting pan. Put into a 300°F preheated oven for one hour to destroy bacteria on the surface. Then adjust the heat to 180–185°F for any size turkey. This is important. The turkey can go in the oven the day before eating it. Example, I have a 22-pound turkey. At 5:00 P.M. Thanksgiving Eve I put the turkey in the oven prepared at 300°F for one hour. I turn the temperature down to 185°F and leave the turkey uncovered until it's done the next day about 10:00 or 11:00 A.M.

Although the cooking times seems startling at first, the meat is amazingly delicious, juicy, and tender. It slices beautifully and shrinks so little that a turkey cooked at regular temperatures no longer tastes good.

It cannot burn so it needs no watching, and vitamins and proteins cannot be harmed at such low heat. It really cooks itself.

A good rule for timing is about three times longer than that of moderate temperature roasting. For example, a 20-pound turkey that normally takes 15 minutes per pound to cook would take five hours. The slow-cook method is three times five so it equals 15 hours to cook on the slow method. A smaller turkey cooks 20 minutes per pound. An 11-pound turkey takes three hours, 40 minutes times three equals 11 hours.

Since the lower temperature requires longer cooking, its use must depend on when you wish to serve your turkey. However, once it's done it will not overcook. You can leave it in an additional three to six hours and it will still be perfect. Thus your roasting can be adjusted entirely to your convenience. Allow yourself plenty of time and let your meat thermometer be your guide to when it's done. Your only problem could be if you didn't put it in soon enough.

It browns perfectly and you'll get wonderful drippings for gravy.

Try it—everyone will praise you and your turkey.

Turkey Carving Tips

Just out of the oven, with juices dripping, the turkey looks and smells wonderful. To graciously serve it from platter to plate, try these carving techniques.

1. Remove the drumstick and thigh by pressing the leg away from the body. The joint connecting the leg to the backbone may snap free. If it doesn't, use a sharp knife and cut the leg from the backbone. Cut dark meat completely from the bone structure by following body contour carefully with a knife.

2. Cut drumsticks and thighs apart by cutting through the joint. Place thighs on a separate plate. It's easy to cut meat if you tilt the drumstick to a convenient angle and slice toward the plate.

3. To slice thigh meat, hold the piece firmly on the plate with a fork. Cut even slices parallel to the bone.

4. Remove half the breast at a time by cutting along the breastbone and rib cage with a sharp knife. Lift meat away from the bone.

5. Place a half breast on a cutting surface and slice evenly against grain of the meat. Repeat with second half of the breast when additional slices are needed. (An optional method is to turn the bird so you can start with the breast of the turkey and make thin slices. When you have sliced all the meat from one side of the bird, you can rotate the bird so you can slice the other side of the turkey.)

Tips for Keeping Leftover Turkey

1. Remove stuffing from the bird while it's still hot. Spoon stuffing into a refrigerator container or casserole. Cover and refrigerate. Use within one to two days.

2. Refrigerate extra gravy in a closed container. Use within two to three days. Gravy does not freeze well if it has been thickened.

3. Leave uncarved meat on the bird. It will stay moister. Wrap bird in enough foil to seal. Place in a large plastic bag. Refrigerate. Use within four to five days.

4. The carcass from the turkey makes an excellent base for hearty soup. Boil in a large pot until meat falls from the bones. Lift out and discard the carcass. Add vegetables and seasoning to the pot. Start early in the morning and by evening you will have a beautiful pot of soup.

Other Helpful Thanksgiving Ideas

1. *Chopped onion without tears*—Take the tears out of preparing onions by chopping them in a blender. Cut an onion in quarters or eighths. Fill the blender halfway with water. Add onion pieces. Push the chop button on and off until the onion is chopped to desired size. Drain onions in a colander. Repeat until you have enough onions for your recipe.

2. *Orange shells*—This is a simple, decorative way to serve yams or sweet potatoes. Cut oranges in half and remove fruit and pulp. Add fruit to holiday punch. Prepare cooked yams or sweet potatoes and spoon into orange shells. Nestle oranges around turkey on the platter. For an extra touch, flute top edges of orange shells with a knife and top with a maraschino cherry or a small marshmallow and place them in the oven until the marshmallow melts.

3. *Unconventional day*—Your family may want to plan a day very different from the traditional family gathering. Your plans might include a trip to the beach (climate permitting), the park, mountains or the desert. You might even have hamburgers and

hot dogs. Be sure to bring along some thoughts of inspiration to share together.

4. *Rent a cabin*—You might consider renting a cabin for the four-day holiday and invite friends and family to share this special period of time with you. Have each family bring their own bedding and supply meals for one day. In the evening you can spend time getting started on some Christmas decorations. A great way to cement family relationships.

5. *Hostess gifts*—If you are going to be a guest in someone's home, plan to take an inexpensive hostess gift. A plate of home-made cookies, stationery, tea towels wrapped with a bow tied around them, or even a new turkey baster are all appreciated gifts.

9

Hanukkah

I am the light of the world; he who follows Me shall not walk in the darkness, but shall have the light of life (John 8:12).

When Observed: Celebrated for eight days, beginning the 25th of the Hebrew month Kislev (November-December)
Earliest Observance: 165 B.C.—Jerusalem

My background being Jewish, I find it only fitting to share what at one time was a very important part of my childhood. Hanukkah or Chanukah—either spelling is correct.

Many Gentiles today do not know what the story of Hanukkah is all about. Perhaps you have Jewish friends or your children have friends at school who practice the Jewish faith. It's a wonderful learning experience to know why and what people are talking about when they say, "I'm Jewish and we celebrate Hanukkah." (A special thanks to Harold Phillips, editor of the Jewish Christian outreach of San Diego, for background information on the history of Hanukkah.)

An Eternal Feast of Light

Hanukkah—the commemoration of a miracle whose story has fascinated and inspired generation after generation of the Jewish people.

Over 20 centuries ago, the land of Judea was under the rule of the Syrian king. For a time, the Jews of Judea were free to practice their customs and observe the laws of the Torah. That is, until the reign of King Antiochus.

Antiochus was determined that all those under his rule believe, as he did, in the multigod religion of the Greeks. He sent his men to Judea to enforce his command and sent soldiers to the temple in Jerusalem. They destroyed the holy Ark and burned the Torah scrolls. They ripped the curtains and smashed the beautiful Menorah. A Greek idol replaced these things on the temple altar. No longer could the Jews worship in their temple, and some gave in to the king.

Near Jerusalem in the town of Modi'in, the leader of the town, Mattathias, rebelled against the king and led many of the townspeople away to the mountains where they hid and organized a small army to fight the Syrians. Mattathias, however, was old and in poor health. Before long he realized that he would not survive to lead his army. Judah, one of his five sons, was appointed as leader and was given the name Maccabee. His army became known as the Maccabees.

They lacked numbers, experience, and weaponry, but they knew their terrain and were able to surprise the king's soldiers several times. More importantly, they were fighting with God for the freedom to practice their faith.

After three years of fighting, they reached Jerusalem and went to the temple. They found it desecrated and in a state of shambles. The fighters became builders and, after much hard labor, the temple was again ready for worship. On the twenty-fifth day of the month of Kislev on the Jewish calendar, the great menorah was again ready to be lit. But only specially purified oil could be used and there was none to be found. A massive search finally yielded only a day's supply. More oil would have to be obtained from the town of Tekoah, but even using the best horse and fastest rider, it would take eight days. Nevertheless, the menorah was lit with the knowledge that the temple would soon be in darkness again until the rider returned with more oil.

The next day, the high priest entered the temple. To his amazement, the menorah was still burning. This continued for eight days until the rider returned with the necessary oil. Before long, everyone had heard about the great miracle: God had provided the light! Man's best efforts would have left him in darkness, but God provided the light!

Menorahs will burn for eight days in countless Jewish homes to commemorate and celebrate Hanukkah, the "Feast of Light." The prophet Isaiah, however, foresaw an even greater miracle of light that was to occur. He proclaimed:

> The people who walk in darkness will see a great light; those who live in a dark land, the light will shine on them. . . . For a child will be born to us, a son will be given to us; and the government will rest on His shoulders; and His name will be called Wonderful Counselor, Mighty God, Eternal Father, Prince of Peace. There will be no end to the increase of His government or of peace . . . (Isaiah 9:2,6,7).

Of course, this passage speaks of the coming of the promised Messiah of Israel. Many Jews anticipate this as a future event. Many more speak of "when the Messiah comes" as more of a joke or legend than an anticipation. But Isaiah foresaw this too and wrote:

> Keep on listening, but do not perceive; keep on looking, but do not understand. Render the heart of this people insensitive, their ears dull, and their eyes dim, lest they see with their eyes, hear with their ears, understand with their hearts, and repent and be healed (Isaiah 6:9,10).

The prophet also foresaw that the Messiah, the Great Light, would be rejected by His own people because of their blindness:

> Who has believed our message? And to whom has the arm of the Lord been revealed? For He grew up before Him like a tender shoot, and like a root out of parched ground; He has no stately form or majesty that we should look upon Him, nor appearance that we should be attracted to Him. He was despised and forsaken of men, a man of sorrows, and acquainted with grief; and like one from whom men hide their face, He was despised, and we did not esteem Him (Isaiah 53:1-3).

But Isaiah did say that at least some of the people would see the Great Light he had prophesied about. God is able to open the eyes of the blind. So it was that some seven centuries after Isaiah's prophecy, a Jewish man by the name of Jochanan (better known by his Greek name, John) was able to proclaim about another Jewish man: "In Him was life; and the life was the light of men" (John 1:4). He was speaking of Yeshua (Jesus) of Nazareth.

It didn't stop with John. For nearly 2000 years now, there has always been a small pocket of Jewish people who have accepted that Jesus—who fulfilled all of Isaiah's Messianic prophecies and hundreds of other Old Testament Messianic prophecies—is the Great Light that God promised. True, the majority of the Jewish community rejects this idea, but didn't Isaiah say this would be the case?

Hanukkah is the celebration of God's miraculous provision of light. The best efforts of man would have left him in darkness, but God provided the light. So it is with the Messiah. Our own best efforts in life still leave us uncertain and without peace concerning our origin, purpose, or final destiny. Man has accomplished many things but, to the extent that we are unable to answer the above three issues, we walk in darkness. This very darkness, Isaiah proclaimed, was to be illumined by the Messiah.

Has this happened to you? Is your "feast of light" only eight days long or do you walk in light all year? Do you understand where you came from, why you're here, and where you are going, or are you still one of "the people who walk in darkness"?

John, the New Testament writer, made this assessment concerning the "light of men" he saw in Yeshua: "And the light shines in the darkness, and the darkness did not comprehend it" (John 1:5). He sounds an awful lot like Isaiah, doesn't he?

There will be two celebrations in December that won't be all they should be. One will be the celebration of Christmas as the day of presents and Santa Claus. The other will be a celebration of God's provision of light for only eight days. Hanukkah commemorates a wonderful miracle and it should be celebrated. But wouldn't it be tragic, though, for you to celebrate only the eight-day Feast of Light and remain blind to the fact that God, through His Son, the Messiah, has provided the greatest miracle—an eternal Feast of Light that can be yours just for the asking? Open your eyes, a Great Light is shining brightly!

Hanukkah Traditions

One of the best parts of this season is the food, especially the potato pancakes called latkes. They are crisp and brown, served with homemade applesauce or sour cream or yogurt.

Latke is a Russian word, meaning flat cake. Making latkes was adopted because the Jews wanted to serve a dish cooked in oil to symbolize the miracle of Hanukkah.

The symbolism behind the pancake is threefold. Made initially of flour and water, they served as a reminder of the food hurriedly prepared for the troops as they went to war. The oil used to prepare the pancakes symbolizes the oil that burned for eight days. The eating of latkes commemorates the liberation from Greek rule.

During the eight days of Hanukkah, latkes are eaten daily. They are a delicacy and quite versatile. They can be served for breakfast, brunch, lunch, dinner, or even as a snack. Plain or fancy, they can be eaten with sugar, yogurt, applesauce, or chicken soup. They can be made with buckwheat or potatoes.

It might be fun to have a Hanukkah party for your family, serve latkes and homemade applesauce, and tell the story of Hanukkah. Perhaps you can have nine candles available or borrow a menorah and show how one candle is lit for every day of Hanukkah. This could be done in an adult Sunday school class, also.

Latkes

5 medium-sized potatoes
2 eggs
1 teaspoon salt or Spike
1 small onion, halved

¼ cup wheat germ
¼ teaspoon white pepper or to taste
⅓ cup vegetable oil

Scrub potatoes well and cut them into cubes. Put one egg, a little of the salt, and half the onion in a blender; add 1 cup of the cubed potatoes. Cover and blend for a few seconds. (Do not overblend or you won't get that desirable "grated" consistency.) Pour most of the mixture into a bowl, but retain some to get the blender started again. Repeat the procedure, adding the other egg, more salt, the other onion half, and the remaining potato cubes. When all are grated, mix in the wheat germ and pepper. In large frying pan, heat oil until it sizzles. Spoon about two tablespoons of the mixture into the frying pan to make each latke. Brown well on both sides; then drain on paper towels. If you would rather not fry them, place latkes on an oiled cookie sheet and bake at 350°F until browned. They are not quite so crispy as the fried, but they are good. Yield: 30 latkes. Serves 30 people.

Emilie's Favorite Applesauce

1½ pounds of tart baking apples (a mixture of different kinds is ideal)
½ teaspoon cinnamon or to taste
¼ teaspoon nutmeg or to taste
½ cup apple juice or apple cider or pineapple juice or water
1 slice lemon

Wash apples but do not peel. Cut up washed apples and place in a pot. Add fruit juice or cider and spices. If you like a thinner sauce, add a little more fruit juice. Bring to a boil; then reduce heat and let simmer for about 10 minutes. Cool; then blend in blender. The best applesauce you ever tasted. Yield: 3 cups. This recipe can be done in a microwave on high for about five minutes. If you don't want to use the blender, cook longer until mushy and whip with a fork. Use a crock pot—cook on low for four to six hours or until apples fall apart. Whip with a fork.

10

Christmas

For today in the city of David there has been born for you a Savior, who is Christ the Lord (Luke 2:11).

When Observed: December 25
Earliest Observance: Early fourth century

Christmas celebrates the birth of Jesus Christ with the message of peace on earth, goodwill toward men. Luke 2:1–7 says:

> Now it came about in those days that a decree went out from Caesar Augustus, that a census be taken of all the inhabited earth. This was the first census taken while Quirinius was governor of Syria. And all were proceeding to register for the census, everyone to his own city. And Joseph also went up from Galilee, from the city of Nazareth, to Judea, to the city of David, which is called Bethlehem, because he was of the house and family of David, in order to register, along with Mary, who was engaged to him, and was with child. And it came about that while they were there, the days were completed for her to give birth. And she gave birth to her first-born son; and she wrapped Him in cloths, and laid Him in a manger, because there was no room for them in the inn.

Although the commercialization of this holiday is frustrating to many, the celebration gives a warm glow at a cold time of the year.

People in a hundred languages sing the joys of Christmas and share their respective countries' traditions. Austria gave us "Silent Night", England contributed the mistletoe ball and wassail; Germany, the Christmas tree; Scandinavia, the Yule candle and Yule log; Mexico, the poinsettia plant. These traditions continue to be celebrated with fresh and innovative ideas.

The Biblical narrative of the birth of Jesus contains no indication of the date that the event occurred. Luke's report, however, that the shepherds were "abiding in the field, keeping watch over their flocks by night," suggests that Jesus may have been born in summer or early fall.

In the third century, efforts were made to determine the actual date of the nativity, but only in the year 336 A.D. was definite mention made of December 25.

The early Puritans in America could not celebrate this day for which there was no biblical sanction. Generally speaking, feelings toward Christmas were divided according to religious denomination.

The diminishing objection to Christmas after 1750 was brought about by the rapid growth of the country as a whole. Alabama was the first state to grant legal recognition to Christmas in 1836. By 1890, all the states and territories had made similar acknowledgement. Christmas is the only annual religious holiday to receive this official and secular sanction.

November and December Weekly Activity Schedule

Be positive and don't let the turkeys get you down. No matter how often we tell ourselves that this year is going to be different, we're going to stop giving so much, eating so much, and expecting so much—it just doesn't seem to happen that way.

Disappointments and expectations seem greater than at any other time of the year. Families are not really the picture perfect photo we see portrayed in magazines and on greeting cards. Hearts are never quite as giving and forgiving as they would like to be. Feelings get hurt and tensions run high.

There is a lot to do, and it's all being added to a schedule which may have been just barely workable before the holidays. Jobs, carpools, meals, laundry, illness, homework, etc. still exist and need attention. (See Exhibit charts at end of book.)

Our world doesn't stop because the calendar says it's holiday time, so be kind to yourself, and ask for help. Keep those goals and expectations realistic and spend time celebrating the part of Christmas that means the most to you. If you don't have time to bake this year and you've always done it, don't do it. Find a good bakery or pay a teen to bake for you.

Second Week in November

It takes so little time to save time. The selection of your Christmas cards can be made in October or the first part of November. The best way is to purchase your cards at the 50%-off discounts after last Christmas. Christmas cards are personal selections and should be thought through. Does it say what you feel as a family; what message do you want to give?

With the rising postal costs, many people have geared down on card giving, due in part to the busy schedules we keep. Because of this, our frequent correspondence has fallen short and contact with close friends subsided. Christmas card sending may be the only news we send or receive all year. Even though it takes time we still hold on to this tradition.

If you send cards, you'll receive them. Nothing takes the stress out of a hectic day in December like sitting down with a letter or note from an old friend. It's a gift in itself.

Keep an updated record. We've provided a Christmas card record chart (see Exhibit F). As you receive your cards, check to see if the return addresses are the same as what you have. Make any changes right away so you are sure to have the correct address for next year.

If you don't want to invest in cards, send postcards. The postage is less and there's room enough for a personal message.

If you have a lot of family news, consider photocopying a letter. This may be important to do the year you've moved, added a new baby, or done something truly newsworthy. Otherwise keep your messages short.

Set up a Christmas card station if room is available or set up a card table and have everything collected in one spot: stamps, colored pens, address labels, address book, etc. You can address your envelopes ahead of time and write notes as you have time here or there. Don't forget to recruit help from the family and work together.

If you have printed cards, write a short note to add a personal touch or have the children sign their names by themselves. Ten minutes of your time to write a note can mean more than a gift. Enclose a photo to friends whom you haven't seen for a year or more. I have an album of Christmas photos from friends. Our stockbroker has become close to Bob over the years and sends us a photo of his two dogs. They don't have children and those dogs are their pride and joy. We look forward to their card each year. We've also watched children grow through Christmas pictures friends have sent.

Nancy Taylor, founder of Traditions Press in South Carolina, designed a beautiful Christmas Memory Book—keeping 25 years of Christmas memories. For each year there is a holiday family photo, the Christmas card sent that year, and a written account of events of the year.

We think these books are so special that we make them available at all our seminars. It makes a perfect wedding gift. If we had started one when we first married, we would be well into our second book. I'll never forget the story of a young bride, Cecila, married to Dr. Dick Patchett, an opthalmologist. She purchased one of our Christmas Memory Books and was so excited as she showed the book to her new husband. He looked it over and then asked, "Where's the second book?" "What do you mean, second book?" bubbled Cecila. "We'll be married more than 25 years and one won't be enough." She quickly got another book.

We take our family Christmas photo every Thanksgiving. That is one time we all seem to be together. It's fun, too, if you can coordinate your clothing. Be creative and do your own thing. Include the pets, teddy bears, and favorite dolls or toys.

Make up your Christmas gift list early in November. Be sure to list everyone you want to remember from the newspaper boy to your dentist. Don't forget anyone who has been special to you and extra helpful that past year.

We've given you a chart to help organize the gift-giving dilemma (see Exhibit B). This helps me to remember who gets what. I do a lot of food and food basket giving. I need that list by my side as I put together my holiday love baskets. You can also refer back to your list to make sure you aren't repeating gifts.

We've also given you a chart for gift records. With all the excitement on Christmas morning, it's hard to remember who gave you what. Keep a record of each gift as it's opened and then, once a thank-you has been written, check the appropriate blank (see Exhibit C).

It's still early November and if you didn't buy your gift wrap after Christmas last year, now is the time to do it. Keep a good supply of scotch tape; gift tags; red, green and white ribbon, and lots of tissue paper.

Gift tags can be made ahead of time from last year's Christmas cards—a great cut-and-paste project for children. Tags can also be made from matching wrapping paper cut into different shapes—stars, angels, teddy bears, squares, hearts, etc.

Continuing the first week in November, you should seriously be purchasing Christmas gifts (see Exhibits A, B, and C), especially those which need to be mailed out of state or out of the country. We'll cover rules for mailing in another section.

November: Week 2—Things to Do

	Activity	Done (x)
1.		☐
2.		☐
3.		☐
4.		☐
5.		☐
6.		☐
7.		☐
8.		☐
9.		☐
10.		☐

Third Week in November

Check your Christmas card list. Update names and addresses and decide if you will send one to everyone you know or just to those people who live out of town.

People will start hunting for gift ideas for you and other members of the family (see Exhibit A). Make your "wish list" for yourself. I really struggle with this, but Bob and the children have no problem making up their list and it's wonderful to know what they want and/or need. I am learning not to be bashful with my wishes. Remember to update sizes for the children when telling grandparents so exchanges are kept to a minimum.

Bake early and freeze food if possible. It will make your last-minute list go a lot easier—rolls, breads, and even some desserts freeze beautifully.

November: Week 3—Things to Do

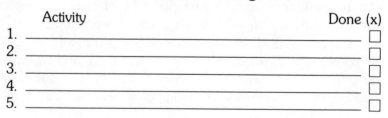

	Activity	Done (x)
1.		☐
2.		☐
3.		☐
4.		☐
5.		☐

6. _____ ☐
7. _____ ☐
8. _____ ☐
9. _____ ☐
10. _____ ☐

Fourth Week in November

It's still the fourth week in November so let's get a good jump on organization.

If you haven't already done so, send out any holiday invitations for parties, potlucks, Christmas teas, open house or any gatherings you are planning. By doing this early, people will make their plans around yours (see Exhibit E).

Advent will begin soon, so if you plan on having an advent wreath with candles or advent calendars for the children get them out now. If you plan to purchase one this year look for a Christ-centered calendar—try your Christian bookstore. Find one that has scriptures and/or tells the Christmas story. As each window is opened, it will give you and the family an opportunity to follow the events leading up to Christ's birth.

Check your church calendar, newspaper or community bulletin for special advent events.

November: Week 4—Things to Do

Activity   Done (x)

1. _____ ☐
2. _____ ☐
3. _____ ☐
4. _____ ☐
5. _____ ☐
6. _____ ☐
7. _____ ☐
8. _____ ☐
9. _____ ☐
10. _____ ☐

First Week of December

Finish up Christmas gift shopping and don't forget the gift wrap, batteries, film, tree ornament hooks, or any other items you might need. Did you remember to put on your gift list a small remembrance for your postal person, receptionist, church secretary, trash man, dentist, doctor, pediatrician, or any other person who has served you well this past year?

Once you have your major purchases made, remind yourself you are finished, so you won't be tempted to buy more than you intended just because you suddenly get the Christmas spirit! Leave some things such as stocking stuffers until the last minute if it makes you happy to be a part of the hustle and bustle.

Pamper yourself. Think about your holiday wardrobe. Does anything need to be cleaned, hemmed, pressed, or altered? Do you need to add new accessories to freshen up the old basic Christmas dress? Schedule a time for a mid-December hair appointment, manicure, or maybe a massage. Do whatever time and finances allow, but you need a rejuvenating experience if at all possible. Try to get plenty of sleep and exercise.

Plan your holiday entertaining menus for Christmas Eve and/ or Christmas Day. If you have room in your freezer, purchase your turkey early. If you are planning on having a fresh turkey, goose, or ham place your order now.

Decide what table linens you'll be using and Scotchguard them; it's a great fabric protector. Spills will be easier to remove.

Keep candles in the freezer until ready for use. That way they don't have a tendency to drip or spark when lit.

Plan several baking days and put these on your calendar. Have at least one day with the children to make those special Christmas cookies and gingerbread men. Mentally you're prepared for the mess—dough, powdered sugar, colored frosting, coconut, and sugar all over the children. Let it be fun for them. How proud they will be when they serve a plate of their own creations.

Your days or evenings of cooking can be spent making and freezing hors d'oeuvres, casseroles, fruitcakes, plum puddings, or anything else which should have time to mellow. Not only will it mellow but you'll feel mellow because you've gotten a good start on a busy holiday.

Begin addressing Christmas cards if you haven't already.

Having trouble with candles standing up? Twist a rubber band around the base before inserting it into the holder. Or keep candles firmly in place by putting a little florist's clay in the holder.

When candles drip on your pretty tablecloths, fear not. Lay a paper towel on the ironing board and place the cloth with the wax spot on top with another paper towel on top of that. Press the wax spot with a medium-to-hot iron. Keep moving the paper towels until the wax is absorbed into them. Presto! The wax is gone and the cloth is saved.

Put up Christmas decorations in the house such as wreaths, garlands, candles, nativity scenes, front door decorations, and bows. String up the outdoor lights. This is a good project for teenagers—they love climbing ladders and getting up on roofs. They could make themselves available to do it for the neighborhood and make extra Christmas money or do it as a ministry to people in the church. A cup of hot cider and Christmas cookies is a good payment for a hardworking, hungry teen.

Review again your list for holiday entertaining and menu planning. Keep feeding the freezer with yummy baked items. What special love gifts these are for friends and neighbors, especially the busy working woman since her time is so limited.

A fun idea is to give a favorite recipe and with it include one or two ingredients. One of my favorites is my triple chocolate cake recipe. Everyone loves it and it's so easy—only three steps and five minutes. This is one I couldn't live without for any last-minute special dessert.

I give the recipe and include a package of chocolate chips, a box of chocolate pudding, and the box of chocolate cake mix.

Emilie's Triple Chocolate Fudge Cake

Prepare 1 sm. package chocolate pudding mix (cooked type) as directed on package. Blend cake mix (dry mix) into hot pudding. Pour into prepared oblong pan, 13" × 9½" × 2". Sprinkle with ½ cup semi-sweet chocolate pieces and ½ cup chopped nuts. Bake 30–35 minutes at 350°F. Serve warm with whipped cream, ice cream, or plain.

Following are great recipes for Christmas Spiced Tea and Holiday Wassail. Make a double batch and divide it into small, attractive jars. Put on a holiday label with instructions and tie a red ribbon around each jar. Your gift recipient will love it and enjoy the special thought for the holiday season.

Christmas Spiced Tea

1 cup instant tea (dry) (can use decaffeinated)
2 cups dry Tang
3 cups sugar (may use 1½ cups sugar substitute and 1½ cups sugar)
½ cup red hots (candy)
1 tsp. cinnamon
½ tsp. powdered cloves
1 pkg. Wyler's lemonade mix

Makes 1½ quarts—to one cup of hot water, add one heaping tablespoon of mix.

Gifts don't have to be expensive. The effort and love that you put into your homemade gifts will be especially appreciated.

Make a batch of bran muffins. You can give the recipe, a muffin tin, and six muffins in the tin. Wrap the tin with clear cellophane wrap, tie a bell and pretty bow on top, and share your love of muffins with your family and friends.

When I have a holiday party, open house, or tea, I serve my Holiday Wassail. It has received lots of compliments and makes the house smell festive and wonderful.

Holiday Wassail Recipe

1 gallon apple cider
1 large can pineapple juice (unsweetened)

¾ cup strong tea—can use herb tea

In a cheesecloth sack put:
    1 Tbsp. whole cloves
    1 Tbsp. whole allspice
    2 sticks cinnamon

This is great cooked in a crockpot. Let it simmer very slow for four to six hours. You can add water if it evaporates too much. Your house will smell wonderful and friends and family will love it!

December: Week 1—Things to Do

Activity   Done (x)

1. _____ ☐
2. _____ ☐
3. _____ ☐
4. _____ ☐
5. _____ ☐
6. _____ ☐
7. _____ ☐
8. _____ ☐
9. _____ ☐
10. _____ ☐

Second Week of December

Finish wrapping your Christmas presents and update your gift list. This will lessen last-minute gift wrapping. Do you have a good hiding place for the children's gifts? If not, consider asking a neighbor to swap hiding places with you.

If you made any catalog purchases, check your orders. Has everything arrived? If not, call the customer service department and inquire. Remember your quiet and gentle spirit! They may be frazzled and not as organized as you are. Shop for necessary gift substitutes or have plan B ready if the order doesn't arrive in time.

The time frame for decorating is a personal or a family decision. We like to have our decorations up for the whole month, so we begin early. Our tree goes up by the second week in December. It may be fun to get a few things out each day for a week or so, culminating your efforts with the trimming of the tree. This makes it easier for the busy woman and fun for the kids, too.

My friend, Ginny Pasqualucci, keeps her decorations up well into January. She loves Christmas so much. Last year she went to the Holy Land for Christmas. They had us over for dinner January 29 for a full Christmas evening complete with Bing Crosby singing "White Christmas," all the decorations still up, and gifts under their two trees. It was wonderful. So do whatever you prefer—it's kosher.

Remember those replacement bulbs. Do you have enough for tree-trimming day, plus ornament hangers for the ornaments?

Make tree trimming a special fun time. Play Christmas tapes and light a few candles if it is during the evening. Make an easy meal, or you could have a cookie-and-hot-spiced-tea platter ready for "halftime." This is a good time to pull out a casserole from the freezer for dinner.

If you are planning a Christmas Eve potluck or buffet, review your menu. This can become a tradition. One week before, each family member can plan a dish to serve. Prepare the dish a day or two ahead. After Christmas Eve services spread out the buffet near the tree on snack tables. You can have a sing-along, read the Bible, and serve communion.

The Christmas breakfast brunch menu, if you're serving one, should be checked. Make sure you have everything you need in your pantry. Are all ingredients available?

Plan your table settings and centerpiece.

December: Week 2—Things to Do

	Activity	Done (x)
1.	_____	☐
2.	_____	☐
3.	_____	☐

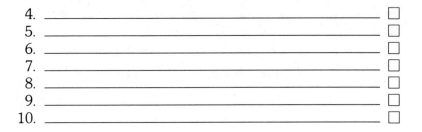

4. _____ ☐
5. _____ ☐
6. _____ ☐
7. _____ ☐
8. _____ ☐
9. _____ ☐
10. _____ ☐

Third Week of December

The countdown continues. Double-check your shopping lists, supplies, menus, etc. You may have parties to attend yourself. Save the invitations until you've written your thank-you notes. Take a baked goodie, some Christmas Spiced Tea, or a handmade ornament as a hostess gift.

If your tree didn't go up last week, this may be the week to put it up. You may want to invite friends to help make it a festive event. String fresh cranberries or popcorn (this takes patience).

Check your holiday calendar for this week and next, including special church services that you will want to attend. Are you beginning to feel overwhelmed—hustled, hurried, and hassled? If so, prioritize events and extend regrets to those you really don't have to attend. You need time for yourself if you are going to enjoy the next two weeks. It's okay to say no.

Make a list of holiday telephone calls you want to make to family and friends and begin making them now. The circuits will be very busy on Christmas Eve and Christmas Day and you don't want to spend all your time dialing the phone.

Many families have a birthday cake for Jesus. This can be made ahead and frozen. One mom shared an idea with her family of having a birthday cake for Jesus complete with candles. They decided to do it after the presents were opened on Christmas morning. Another family has their party very simply at the end of Christmas Day—packages all opened, paper everywhere, and dirty dishes. They take ten minutes and sing "Happy Birthday, Jesus," blow out the candles, and have a quiet family communion. The eating of the cake is not what is important. That can be done another day if tummies are too full. The purpose is to focus on the real meaning of Christmas.

December: Week 3—Things to Do

	Activity	Done (x)
1.		☐
2.		☐
3.		☐
4.		☐
5.		☐
6.		☐
7.		☐
8.		☐
9.		☐
10.		☐

Christmas Week

Not much to do—we have our plan and the plan is working.

Go over the menus and supplies one more time. Any last-minute purchases necessary? Shop for groceries.

Try to keep normal routines, if possible, because small children sense the excitement and can be overwhelmed. Schedule reading times with them. Our grandchildren love the Christmas story all year long—they love to hear it over and over. Talk about what the true meaning of Christmas is—how we give gifts just as the wise men brought gifts to the Christ child.

Place the wrapped gifts under the tree, if you haven't already done so. If you open most of the gifts on Christmas Day, consider letting each child open one early. It may be the most appreciated.

Keep that list of gifts received up-to-date as each present is opened. This makes writing thank-you notes much easier.

Check your stocking-stuffer items and have them ready to fill on Christmas Eve—late. If Santa comes to your house, leave a snack for him and don't forget a carrot for Rudolph!

Set your Christmas Eve and/or Christmas Day tables a few

days ahead. Put out those serving dishes labeled with the 3 × 5 cards.

Relax and enjoy yourself and your family. Have a very Merry Christmas. You've worked hard and planned well. You deserve a blessed Christmas.

December: Week 4—Things to Do

	Activity	Done (x)
1.	_____	☐
2.	_____	☐
3.	_____	☐
4.	_____	☐
5.	_____	☐
6.	_____	☐
7.	_____	☐
8.	_____	☐
9.	_____	☐
10.	_____	☐

Parcel Post Shipping Hints

This is the time of year when post office lobbies draw crowds.

The U.S. Postal Service's first rule at this time of year is "the earlier the better." Here are additional tips for insuring that your mail arrives in time for the holidays:

1. *Containers*—The postal service says fiberboard boxes, such as those available at grocery stores and other retailers, are ideal. Popular sized boxes and mailing envelopes or bags are available at stationers and post office branches.

2. *Packing*—Cushion box contents with crumpled newspaper. Place the paper around all sides, corners, top, and bottom so the contents won't move, even if you shake the box. Foam shells, "popcorn," and padding are sold for cushioning and may be worth the investment if the items you're planning to send are particularly fragile. Mark the package if the contents are fragile in

three places: above the address, below the postage, and on the reverse side.

Padded mailing envelopes or bags are ideal for small items including books. Avoid using twine, cord, or string. No wrapping paper is allowed on the outside of packages. With boxes, brown paper is not necessary. Put a slip of paper with name and address of the recipient inside the box as well as addressing it on the outside.

3. *Sealing*—Close the carton with one of the three recommended types of tape: pressure-sensitive, nylon-reinforced paper, or glass-reinforced pressure sensitive. No Scotch tape, please!

4. *Addressing*—Use smudge-proof ink. Put the recipient's name and address in the lower right portion of the package. Cover the label with clear tape to waterproof. Put your return address in the upper left corner of only one side of the package. Remove all other labels from the box. Use zip codes—wrong zip code can delay delivery.

5. *Christmas cards*—Holiday cards must be standard size envelopes at least 3½ inches high and 5 inches long. If the card is extra large, you will have to pay added postage. If in doubt, have it measured by a postal clerk.

Mail not only early in the month, but early in the day. If you are mailing across the continent, the U.S. Postal Service advises allowing eight to ten days for packages and cards.

Find shipping boxes, wrap, and ship all out-of-state Christmas gifts, if possible, before December 1.

When mailing a gift-wrapped present, stuff the package into a dry cleaner plastic bag with crumpled newspaper to be used as buffers with packing. The newsprint won't rub off on the wrapping paper. Protect the bow from being crushed by covering it with a plastic berry basket—the type strawberries come in.

Surviving the Stress of Shopping

The busy woman today doesn't even want to think about Christmas until after Thanksgiving; we simply haven't had the time to get into stores to shop. We have had meetings to attend and deadlines to meet. The teacher whose energies went into the classroom and who postponed shopping until school was out is now faced with a dilemma. Even the retailers who have been so busy selling to others haven't had time themselves to buy. We all share the common expression, "Help!" However, there is hope. Organization is the key to the task. We all have limited time. Every minute you spend in the stores must have a purpose. Before you begin, plan your shopping strategy.

1. In your mind review all the stores in a center or mall. Perhaps a better idea is to write them down—bookstore, china shop, hardware store, jewelry store, clothing shop, etc. Hopefully you can accomplish the majority of your shopping in one trip.

2. Make a list based on the shops within a particular mall. Work your way around mentally, jotting down specific people.

3. Take advantage of wrapping services and/or gift boxes, ribbon, and tissue. Have as many gifts as you can ready to place under the tree when you arrive home.

4. Do two things at once. If, for example, you purchase clothing for three people which includes gift wrapping, allow the clerks to finish the packages while you visit other shops. Circle back at the end of the day and collect your packages.

5. Decide before you go out if this year you are purchasing "one big gift" or lots of little things. Each year I do things a bit differently.

6. Give something an unusual touch. For example, if you are giving a cookbook, wrap it in a tea towel or add an apron or muffin tin. If it's a piece of jewelry, include a nightshirt. Compress your gift into a can or a jar.

7. Think in categories: How many golfers, skiers, and tennis players are on your list? If buying for one, buy for three. What about duplicate gifts? Can you give all your neighbors a soup mix or the gourmet cheese or spiced-mustard jar? Absolutely! Many times one stop will take care of five or six gifts.

8. You can also use the phone to your advantage. Call your florist to make up a unique silk arrangement basket of soaps and hand cream, etc. They will often wrap and deliver the baskets for you. Anyone would love to receive a pretty holiday arrangement

with a candle for the Christmas table centerpiece.

9. For the hard-to-please and those people who have every-thing, a gift certificate for a restaurant, ice cream shop, or fast-food restaurant (children love that) are always a hit.

10. Take a few breaks during your shopping to renew your list and thoughts. Plan a coffee, tea, or lunch break. You will also need to make periodic trips to lock the packages in your car.

11. Don't leave the shopping area until you are sure you have accomplished all you wanted to do in that spot. Retracing your steps or making second trips isn't really practical at a late date.

12. Ask a teenager or even a friend who loves to shop to pick something up for you.

13. Remember to keep it simple. The love you put into each gift will be what lasts. This season is the time for warmth, fellow-ship, shared experiences, and hospitality.

Blessings for a beautiful holiday filled with joy!

How to Keep Holidays Stressless

Here are a few more hints and tips to keep your holidays stressless:

1. Ask your family members to share their favorite holiday memory. You may be surprised how few meals and toys they mention. We did this at our church Christmas party one year and, to my surprise, very few of them could recall special holiday mem-ories. If this be the case, create some memories. Make your time count—a memory lasts forever, but toys get broken.

2. Try not to do everything yourself. Small children can help, just lower your perfection a little and allow those small hands to bake and decorate. These experiences may stay in their memories long after the holidays are over. Even if your husband is unable to help you the rest of the year, the Christmas spirit will inspire him. Ask him to help you or ask if he could run some errands near where he works.

3. Settle family matters ahead of the holiday time. Families are often separated by divorce or geographic distance and disputes can arise. Try to make all the arrangements well ahead

of time. If you have out-of-town guests, decide where they will stay and let them know before they arrive if they really need to be at a motel. Share your time equally and fairly with each set of grandparents or take turns from year to year. Avoid overcommitment—it can make for situations where people are overtired and overreact.

4. Don't gain weight. Feeling fat in party clothes can really add to your stress and tension. Overeating can make you feel absolutely awful. Try to schedule the same exercise you normally do. If you are not exercising now make it a goal for the new year.

There will be a great deal of extra goodies around, but be selective about what you eat. Stick to the things that are worth it, like your favorites that you see only at holiday time.

Place yourself next to the food table where the fruit or veggie platter is. If you decide now not to overdo it, you won't have to make that New Year resolution to lose weight later.

5. Remember what really matters. As Christians, Christmas is the time for celebrating the birth of Christ and everything else comes after that special celebration. The hassles will take care of themselves.

6. Watch your finances carefully. Talk about tension and depression! Overspending will do it, especially if you've overcharged and have those bills to look forward to later. Ask the Lord to help you in this area so you won't get caught up in the spirit of things and buy much more than you budgeted for.

Remember that a handmade gift or baked item can be more valuable than an expensive one. Special phone calls or a coupon for an "after Christmas lunch treat" can mean as much to a friend as an expensive gift they may not use or like. Set your budget and stick to it. Many people have a special Christmas fund set aside. That makes it easy and when that's gone, it's gone. Otherwise, spread your purchases over a period of time and charge only the amount you intend to spend. That's why we suggest you begin your gift shopping early in November so it doesn't all come at once.

7. It's okay to say no. You'd like to do it all, be everywhere, and see everything. But for today's busy woman, it just can't be.

Don't be afraid to say "No, we need this time together as a family" or "No, I can't bake the extra cookies but I'd be happy to buy some." Don't feel guilty about those things you simply can't do.

8. Plan some time for yourself. You can read a book, listen to a tape or music, take a bubble bath with a candle lit, get a good haircut, have your nails polished, or maybe even buy yourself a new nightgown, blouse, or holiday sweater. By taking care of yourself, that last-minute hassle about your appearance won't happen.

9. Christmas will come regardless if you've done everything on your lists or not. Do those things which really matter and let the others fall where they may.

Family, friends, and above all the true meaning of Christmas is what counts. Remember: 60% of our stress is caused by disorganization.

Decorating and Entertaining Ideas

The most important entertaining you will do during the year, and especially the Christmas season, will be for your own family. In our home it's a special time for all of us. I bring out what china, crystal, and silver I have just for these family times. The children have learned to handle the dishes gently and it makes for treasured learning times.

1. *Sheets for tablecloths*—I have fun mixing and matching my table settings. Here are a few ideas I use to make my tables creative and different. Regardless of what the holiday may be, I use sheets for making tablecloths and napkins. I'll take the saucer from my set of eight dishes to the store to look for sheets that might match or coordinate. Many times I'll find a sheet on sale that will work perfectly. I keep my eyes open all year for white sales and I've found some great bargains.

To make one tablecloth for a standard-size table and get 12 napkins, use a king size sheet (flat). If you don't want so many napkins or have a small table, you can use a full or queen-size sheet. A twin sheet will do if you don't want matching napkins. (You can make six napkins out of one yard of coordinating fabric.

Cut each napkin 15" square.) It is quite alright to leave the border on the tablecloth if you wish. People don't usually go around to see if you have a border on the side.

Measure the length and width of your table and add six inches to hang over each side. Then add one inch for a turn-under hem. Cut your tablecloth out first, either open flat or folded in half, whichever you wish. Then fit your napkins out of the remainder. A nice size for napkins is 18" square, but you may want a smaller napkin.

If you are making a round tablecloth, fold the sheet in half and cut a string the radius of your table plus the six-inch drop and one-inch hem and mark your cutting line with pins or chalk into your half circle. You can cut your napkins out right next to each other using the same cut. It's always nice to finish the napkins with lace or eyelet embroidery.

I continue to look for Christmas sheets but so far haven't found any with poinsettias, holly, or red-and-green prints or stripes. Many times I have to settle for holiday fabric such as taffeta, felt, or even lace panel curtains. I bought a lace panel curtain at K-Mart for $5.99 one year and made a tablecloth. I also made six napkins and one lace runner from it.

A green or red felt fabric tablecloth is great for Christmas. You can buy felt by the yard. It doesn't have to be hemmed, and it's nice and wide so no sewing is needed. Also today's new felt is completely washable. It looks beautiful as is or you can add a plaid runner, taffeta over-cloth, or even holiday placemats. Napkin rings can be made with taffeta ribbon by tying a bow around the napkin.

2. *Napkin Rings*—Cover empty toilet paper rolls with lace and cut the rolls 2–3" in width for simple but nice napkin rings.

Paint wooden clothespins red, green, or white. Names can be personalized with a paint pen from the craft store.

Using quilted fabric, cut a boot, star or angel leaving an opening at the top for a napkin. The fabric can be sewn or glue-gunned together.

Cookie cutters (plastic or metal) make great napkin rings. You can find them in gourmet stores, kitchen sections of department stores, and catalogs. They come in all shapes.

Napkin rings can be made out of many different materials. One year we were having 26 people for our family Christmas dinner. I was using an old standby poinsettia fabric tablecloth I'd used previously, but I wanted to jazz it up a bit. I found some wooden napkin rings, cheap! I bought some red silk poinsettia flowers (small version), cut off the long stem, and glue-gunned the flower to the plain wooden rings. It was sensational with my green napkins, but the best part was I had 26 matching napkin rings for less than 25 cents each. I've used them for the past four years. They store well and keep their shape as long as I put them in my numbered storage boxes.

If you want to go fancy, start collecting china napkin rings. Buy two to four each year until you have enough for your table or let your family know you're collecting them. It's a great gift idea.

Here's an idea for a Christ-centered napkin ring. Take your paper towel tube and cut it in two-inch widths. Then cut it so it opens. Write a scripture inside and with your glue gun or regular glue cover the outside with ribbon leaving tails long enough on each side to tie a bow. Slide your napkin through the ring. When your family or guest untie the bow, there in front of their eyes will be God's Word. You can have each person read their verse and it can become the prayer of blessing.

3. *China collection*—Thirty-two years ago when Bob and I were married, I shared with my family that I would like to collect china cups and saucers. Since that time, I have received over 30 gifts of beautiful cups and saucers, all different. I use them often, letting our guests pick out a favorite they'd like to use that evening. I have several different dinner plates that don't match also, and it's so much fun to set a table with all the different plates and cups. It's become a conversation piece. I've also found some great buys on china plates at garage and estate sales. It's a fun hobby, and I use the plates and cups often.

I found a terrific buy at a bargain store. They were selling solid red ceramic plates at 88 cents each. I use these red plates for Christmas with the green felt tablecloth and the red poinsettia napkin rings. The red plates come out again for Valentine's Day with pink and white napkins and again on the Fourth of July for our red, white, and blue patio party. It's been a great investment.

4. *Centerpieces*—For a centerpiece, it's attractive to arrange several different size candles at different heights, maybe six to ten candles. When lit, they make a beautiful effect and yet it is so simple.

Tie a plaid Christmas bow around the base of your candles or around the candle holder itself. You can change the ribbons and bows for all seasons and holidays.

A pretty centerpiece is a wreath set on a glass plate on the table with candles in the center. Use your creativity with pinecones, poinsettias, flowers, ribbon, moss, ivy, and holly.

Make small stuffed teddy bears in Christmas fabrics. Christmas trees and gingerbread men are cute, too. Tie a bow around the neck of each bear. These can be placed against each person's water glass as a gift to remember the evening in your home.

Teddy bears are universal and versatile. They can be used for hugging, loving, and sharing. To make the bears, I take scraps of leftover holiday fabric or buy remnants and cut out the bears (see Exhibit G). Stuff with fiberfill or use cotton. You'll need to make at least a dozen. Put a red or green bow around their neck. Then write a Scripture verse on a piece of paper and roll it up and insert it through the ribbon around teddy's neck. Not only do your guests take home a teddy bear, but they also take home God's Word.

Ideas for Holiday Leftovers

My very favorite part of a big Christmas dinner is the leftovers. I'll cook a turkey just for that purpose. There is something about the taste of cold turkey snitched in the kitchen on Christmas night or later in the week that is better than any feast ever served in a four-star restaurant. In fact, some of the best meals I've served all year have been the result of holiday leftovers. Here are some special tips for using those leftovers:

1. Freshen rolls by sprinkling with water and heating in the oven, adding butter and garlic powder if desired.

2. Make TV dinners by placing leftovers in an aluminum pan, covering with foil, and labeling before sticking in the freezer. Perfect for busy days and late suppers.

3. Leftover food should be stored within two hours, which includes serving time. Keep hot foods hot (above 165°F) and cold foods cold (below 40°F).

4. Freeze leftover gravy in ice cube trays; pop out cubes and store in plastic bags. Do the same with fruit juices.

5. Freeze leftover water chestnuts tightly covered in their liquid.

6. Bits of jelly and jam can be melted in a small pan over low heat to make a good sauce for waffles, puddings, or ice cream. This also makes a nice glaze.

7. Avoid storing different cakes, cookies, or breads in the same container. The flavors mix and the baked goods don't keep as well.

8. To refresh cookies that are too soft, heat in a 300°F oven just before serving. If cookies are too hard, place them in an airtight container and add a piece of apple or bread. It will take a day or two to soften them.

9. Cooked meats and vegetables should just be reheated and added at the end of cooking or assembling a casserole. This helps retain flavor, texture, and nutritional value.

Holiday Storage

It's over—now what?

Storage can be a very easy process and will relieve stress for next year when done properly.

Here's what you'll need:

- A good supply of white "perfect boxes"—16" long by 12" wide by 10" deep with a flip-top lid.
- 1 black felt pen
- 3 × 5 card file box
- 3 × 5 cards

CHRISTMAS

Instead of writing all over the "perfect" box with a description of the contents, simply number your boxes #25A, #25B, #25C, etc. (25 for the 25th of December). Then make out a 3 × 5 card numbering the Box #25A, #25B, #25C, etc. On the left corner of your card, wirte the area where the box is stored. Example: garage, attic, cellar, closet in spare room, guest bedroom. List on the card exactly what you are storing in each numbered "perfect" box. These cards can be stored in a 3 × 5 file box. When you need an item, just look it up in your file box and go to the storage area where the "perfect" box is. It's easy, quick, and neat.

Keep your strings of lights tangle-free by storing them inside an empty toilet paper or paper towel roll. Or wrap them around the outside of the empty paper towel roll.

We have 12 filled "perfect" boxes, four marked trash baggies, and four oversized boxes that all have 25A, 25B, etc. labeled on them. As you can tell, Christmas is big in our home. But when December comes, it's a neat, easy process. I don't have boxes and baggies all over the garage floor for the whole month. I take down what I need, when I need it. In August when I begin to prepare for our holiday seminars (which begin mid-October), I can take those items down from the garage shelves and look through my table cloths, napkins, and props and freshen up those things that need attention. I can add new items and ideas to the old and it's as easy as pumpkin pie. You'll actually be excited about storage.

One woman wrote:

The ideas in your Holiday Seminar changed our lives, especially the section on storage. We did exactly as you said and filled our boxes, labeled by numbers, and when my husband saw how beautiful they looked he built shelves so they would fit perfectly on them. But we didn't stop there. We decided to clean out the basement and boxed everything up. You should see how excited we get when we need something. We go right to our little file box and find what we need on the card and pull the box. It has saved us so much time and frustration. Thank you, Emilie, for all your great ideas. We're on box #36 and still adding.

Bless you,
Flo—Kentucky

It's letters like that, that make our ministry so rewarding.*
Garlands, wreaths, and candles should be stored separately
from ornaments. That way, next year you can start your holiday
decorating without sorting through boxes of tree decorations.
Large items such as wreaths can be stored in plastic trash bags
labeled as if they were boxes by stapling a 3 x 5 card to the bag.

Traditions

Whether you've had traditions in your past or not, you can
begin to implement them in your own home, making a rich heritage for you and your children that can be passed on from generation to generation. It's not too late to start now. It makes no
difference whether you're a family or an individual, you can still
create memories and establish traditions. It's our responsibility to
create good family memories and traditions that can be handed
down to our children and our children's children. Psalm 71:17–
21 says:

> O God, Thou hast taught me from my youth; and I still
> declare Thy wondrous deeds. And even when I am old and
> gray, O God do not forsake me, until I declare Thy strength
> to this generation, Thy power to all who are to come. For Thy
> righteousness, O God, reaches to the heavens, Thou who
> hast done great things; O God, who is like Thee? Thou, who
> hast shown me many troubles and distresses, wilt revive me
> again, and wilt bring me up again from the depths of the earth.
> Mayest Thou increase my greatness, and turn to comfort me.

Dr. James Dobson points out:

> The great value of traditions comes as they give a family
> a sense of identity, a belongingness. All of us desperately need
> to feel that we're not just a cluster of people living together in
> a house, but we're a family that's conscious of its uniqueness,
> its personality, character and heritage, and that our special

*For more detailed information on all-year storage, you may want to refer to Emilie's
chapter entitled "Total Mess to Total Rest" *Survival For Busy Women* (Harvest House).

relationships of love and companionship make us a unit with identity and personality.

1. *Cookie exchange*—This is a great idea. Who invented it? We're not really sure, but it was definitely a woman with a busy schedule and truly a stroke of genius! Instead of spending a fortune on ingredients and lots of time making a variety of cookies for the holidays, you can make a large batch of your favorites and swap them for many different kinds.

One of the most fun times I had was at a cookie exchange one morning with our church women. We had hot apple cider and lots of fellowship (now this could be done in an evening or with husbands). I received an invitation that instructed me to bring seven dozen cookies plus my recipe written on a recipe card that would be displayed by my cookie plate.

Our hostess had a lovely table prepared with candles for displaying our cookies. She prepared the hot cider and extra recipe cards for those of us who wanted to record the other recipes. We were each given a paper tote bag (or it could be a box or tray) for taking cookies home. The tote bags added an extra touch. They aren't expensive and we felt like kids in a candy store filling our bags.

Each one of us then took an equal number of each kind of cookie. We had a great time and went home with enough variety to please our families—not to mention some great recipes.

2. *Christmas cards*—Our Christmas cards begin to arrive early in December. We read and enjoy them at the moment. I then tear off the return address and check it with my address book to keep it current. The card then goes into our Christmas card basket I decorate with a holiday bow, holly, or a poinsettia. Our basket begins to fill up and it stays where it's visible to the family.

After Christmas this is the one thing we don't store away in boxes, at least not yet. Beginning January 1, we take our card-filled basket to our meal table and before or after our meal each member of the family draws out a card. We read the card and who it is from and then offer a prayer for that person or family. This tradition can last well into the new year. Many times I'll drop a note to the family saying, "Thank you for your Christmas card. Our family read it today, March 6, and we prayed for you. Blessings from our home to yours!"

3. *Family movies, videos, slides*—It's so much fun to see those old family movies, slides, or photos. Today's family, however, can videotape, so set aside an evening to do just that. It's great to see how everyone has changed.

4. *Communion*—Christmas Eve or after the Christmas day festivities are over, gather your family together and take turns sharing the meaning of that Christmas. The Christmas story can be read and then plan a family communion. A good ending might be to sing "Joy To The World."

5. *Being a witness*—Invite adult friends and/or children's friends to your home to share a December evening with dinner or dessert. Plan songs, games, some pertinent Scripture, and let them observe your example of Christ's love and the atmosphere of love in your home. Your family can follow up with prayer for them during the holiday season and into the new year.

6. *Tree cutting*—In some parts of the United States you can go to a tree farm and choose and cut your own tree. We do this every year. It's become a fun tradition. In our family we have two perfectionists: our son, Brad, and our son-in-law, Craig. We plan a time to go when they can go with us so we're sure to bring home the perfect tree! Some tree farms have picnic areas, small zoos, and even caroling. After we've chosen the tree, we'll go for a picnic or simple dinner or perhaps come home to cookies and hot cider, or maybe chili or hot soup. This creates a memory and brings family togetherness. If no tree farms are available in your area, the tree lot will serve the same purpose. It is also fun to take a picture of your tree untrimmed and then one after it's trimmed. You may not trim your tree the day you purchase it. If not, keep it in a bucket of water or wet sand. Hose it down to wash off the dust and dirt. It will keep well until the time to bring it into the house and trim.

Tree Trimming Party

1. Special food—make it simple: tamales, tacos, hamburgers, pizza, make-your-own Sloppy Joes, spaghetti, Mexican

mountains (make-your-own tostadas), etc.

2. The family can make tree ornaments by using the following: macrame, paper, popcorn, noodles, straw, pipe cleaners, starch, egg shells, paper plates, popsicle sticks, tinsel, aluminum pans, paint, wooden spools, clothes pins, string, fabric, cookies or cranberries. Another idea is to personalize ornaments with a photo or date.

One Christmas we went to the mountains around Lake Tahoe, California, with another family. We decided to take no gifts, no tree ornaments—everything had to be homemade. We purchased a small tree and set up a card table in the center of the living room area. With Elmer's glue, many shapes of noodles, popcorn, cranberries, pinecones, pods, and whatever else nature provided, we each used our creativity to make ornaments. The Christmas music was playing, a roaring fire was in the fireplace, and all our small children were gluing to their little hearts' delight. Those ornaments came home with us and appeared on future Christmas trees until the last ornament finally fell apart.

For our Christmas gifts we took the children and we all went to a local thrift shop. We bought little Michael a small two-wheel bicycle for $2.00. Brad received a football helmet and jersey for $1.50, Jenny a bathrobe, and on and on. What fun as we beautifully wrapped our treasures and celebrated Christ's birthday for under $10.

Baby Jesus

This tradition is probably the sweetest and most meaningful of all. My friend Debbie Hogan of Newport Beach, shared this with me once, and we've done it ever since. She wrote this poem to explain the tradition:

The Manger

The time grows near: let's all rejoice. Christmas morn will soon be here.

God has made His perfect choice, the baby Christ's birth
is near.
As each day passes, let's make it our goal, to prepare a
comfy bed.
So when the time comes He'll have a place to rest His
tiny head.
We'll add a single piece of straw for each good deed we've
done
To fill the manger to the top while having a lot of fun
Until at last the morning comes we've all been waiting for
And in the bed we've made for Him, lies Jesus Christ the
Lord.

Debbie wrote this poem in calligraphy and framed it. She
then placed it by a manger scene, homemade of birch branches.
(It could be purchased or made of wood or ceramic.) Everything
is displayed except the baby Jesus—hide Him away, but be sure
to remember where. Next to the empty manger is a pile of straw
cut into six-inch pieces. Beginning the first week in December,
we gather as a family and talk about the manger and straw. Every
day each member of the family does a good deed on his or her
own, such as sharing toys happily, helping teacher pass out papers, or taking out trash without being asked. Then, on their
honor, they put a piece of straw in the manger. It could be done
at the end of each day. Make sure to talk about the happiness
they have given to one another.

As the month continues, the straw in the manger grows and
soon a cozy bed of straw fills the manger. Still no baby Jesus
appears. On Christmas Eve, after all the children are nestled in
their beds and asleep, Mom and Dad will find baby Jesus and
place Him in His rightful spot. Straw or no straw, baby Jesus
always appears. Some years the manger may not be real cozy,
but we've found that December is the best month of all for good
behavior. Watch the excitement as the children on Christmas
morning race to see that the baby Jesus has arrived. They head
straight for the manger even before the tree. Why? Because during the month we have been focusing on the real meaning of
Jesus' birthday.

Other Christmas Traditions

We had dinner with some friends one evening and as we walked up to their front door we saw a banner in the window which said "Happy Birthday, Jesus." I really loved that! It takes commitment to do something like that. They also had a birthday party for Jesus with cake, candles, and singing. What a beautiful expression of love for the children to experience. Here are a few more ideas to go along with your party:

- Invite neighborhood children and let them be a part of this special birthday party.
- Bring gifts or food which can be given to a needy family.
- Make craft items with a cross or sign of the fish, such as a puffed, stuffed fabric heart which can be used as a necklace. Let the children wear these gifts home.
- Make bread-dough hearts, personalize them with a paint pen, or paint Love, Joy, Peace, etc. on them and use as tree ornaments at home.
- Older children and adults can share testimonies.
- Share memorable Christmases.
- Have communion with friends.

Our friends Bob and Yoli Brogger probably do the best job of making Christmas memories. Their goal is to glorify Jesus during the month of December. Here are a few of their Christ-centered ideas.

Yoli made a promise candle out of an oatmeal box. She covered the box with red felt then with yellow felt cut a piece in the shape of a flame and glued it onto the top. It looks just like a candle. They fill the box with Scripture promises. Each day of December every member of the family draws out a promise and reads it around the table or at bedtime.

They purchased a Christ-centered Advent calendar (one with Scriptures). You can also make these yourself. Each evening after dinner or before bedtime the family gathers together and opens the appropriate window and reads the Scripture for that day.

The Brogger family also has an Advent candle. These are available through "More Hours In My Day" seminars. Or you can use a regular candle and pretend there are numbers written on the side. Each day of December light the candle for about five minutes. We call it our holiday worship time:

1. The candle is lit.
2. The Advent calendar is opened.
3. A promise is picked from the promise candle and read.
4. The baby Jesus manger tradition can be talked about and also at this time straw can be added.
5. Close with a short prayer.

The candle is then blown out. By Christmas Eve the candle will have burned down. This is a special event in the Brogger home and as the children have grown older they take the leadership part.

From the moment our friends approach our front door we want them to know that within our home we celebrate something special. I have a grapevine wreath and in the center of this beautiful wreath I put a small nativity scene. Each year I make a few changes of ribbon, pinecones, or holly, but I always leave on the nativity scene. As people stand waiting at our door they can't help but look upon what the real meaning of Christmas is.

Christmas stockings are always a lot of fun and can be handmade or store-bought. Again, the Brogger family does a very creative thing. They hang a "joy" stocking. During the month of December each family member puts thoughts, prayers, and love notes in the "joy" stocking. Then on Christmas Eve or Christmas Day they are pulled out and read. This would also be a great idea to do all year around.

Singles can even start traditions. Why not have a party for unmarrieds and include a spiritual emphasis? Light the candles for five minutes and have a little Advent worship time, or read Scripture of your own each day of the month leading up to the twenty-fifth.

Christmas will be as special or as ordinary as you make it. You can be the architect of memories your children will carry with them for years—not just strengthening the bond of family, but deepening their spiritual ties as well. One of the most exciting things about traditions is that we can include others in them, even if they're not Christians. People aren't offended if everything is done in love and with a soft and gentle spirit. The Word that is read and vocalized during the month of December is going into the heart. God is honoring all the prayers we've prayed over Christmas meals and Scriptures we've read over the years:

> And you shall love the Lord your God with all your heart and with all your soul and with all your might. And these words, which I am commanding you today, shall be on your heart; and you shall teach them diligently to your sons and shall talk of them when you sit in your house and when you walk by the way and when you lie down and when you rise up (Deuteronomy 6:5–7).

Advent

Our family sought as many ways as possible to celebrate a Christ-centered Christmas, to create memories that would be everlasting and that our children would carry on into their homes.

One thing my family always remembers about Christmas is my husband opening his Bible, with the Advent candles lit, and reading Scripture. Every Christmas Day at some point Bob will read the Christmas story once again. These are the memories that last forever.

The Advent Wreath

Rich in Christian tradition and symbolism, the Advent wreath brings beauty, light, and truth to our holiday season. The word "advent" means "coming." In all 39 books of the Old Testament, there is the air of expectancy. Someone is coming! During the

133

Advent season, we anticipate the coming celebration of the birth of our Savior.

Advent begins on the fourth Sunday before Christmas and ends on Christmas Eve. A red or purple candle, symbolizing royalty, is lit on each of these four Sundays, and is traditionally accompanied by Scripture reading. The white candle is lit on Christmas Eve, signifying Christ's arrival. The color white speaks of the purity of our Lord. With the lighting of this last candle, the circle is complete just as we are complete in Christ.

The circle of the wreath reminds us that His Kingdom will have no end (Luke 1:33) and that God Himself has no beginning and no end. He has always existed and always will!

The evergreens tell us that Jesus brings eternal life:

> For God so loved the world, that He gave His only begotten Son, that whoever believes in Him should not perish, but have eternal life (John 3:16).

A white dove on the wreath reminds us that the Holy Spirit descended as a dove.

However plain or elaborate your wreath, remember that God's Word is true. He loves you and He sent His only Son into the world that you might have life and have it abundantly (John 10:10)!

Family Advent Worship Time

The Lord is my light and my salvation (Psalm 27:1).

Many families have established the Advent wreath as a wonderful tradition during their Christmas season. Here are some guidelines you may want to use:

1. Make a wreath using straw, evergreens, ribbon, etc. and place four red candles and one white candle around it.
2. Fourth Sunday before Christmas—Light the first

candle. Share verses Isaiah 2:1–5; 11:1–9; 40:3–11 showing the coming of the Messiah.

3. Third Sunday before Christmas—Light the second candle. Share verses Luke 1:26–56; Isaiah 7:13,14 telling of the mother of Jesus.

4. Second Sunday before Christmas—Light the third candle. Share verses Luke 2:8–20, telling about the shepherd and angels. Share Matthew 2:1–12 telling about the wise men.

5. Last Sunday before Christmas—Light the fourth candle. Share Matthew 2:13–23, telling of the flight into Egypt.

6. On Christmas Eve—Light the white and last candle. You may enjoy reading the Christmas story found in Luke 1:26–38 and Luke 2:1–20. Let the candles continue to burn until bedtime.

7. Rejoice—It's the birthday of the King! "I am the light of the world" (John 8:12).

Involve the family and take turns lighting and blowing out the candles. We believe this celebration of Christmas is pleasing to the Lord. It has taught our children the meaning of Christmas and helps us all to remember His birth and feel His presence in our home.

Scripture Reading for the Advent Wreath

The prophecies concerning Christ in the Old Testament which are expressly cited in the New Testament number more than 300! Here are just a few to choose from to add substance to the lighting of your Advent candles.

Prophecy	Fulfillment
Genesis 3:15	Galatians 4:4; Matthew 1:18
Psalm 72:10	Matthew 2:1–11
Psalm 118:26	Matthew 21:9
Isaiah 7:14	Matthew 1:18; Matthew 1:22,23

Isaiah 9:6,7 . . . . John 1:19–34
Isaiah 11:1–10 . . . . Luke 1:26–38
Isaiah 25:8. . . . . 1 Corinthians 15:54
Isaiah 28:16 . . . . Romans 9:33; 1 Peter 2:6
Isaiah 35:4–6 . . . . Matthew 11:4–6; John 11:47
Isaiah 40:3–5 . . . . Matthew 3:3; Mark 1:3; Luke
                                              3:4–6
Isaiah 53:3–6,9,12 . . . . Acts 26:22,23; 1 Peter 2:22;
                                              Luke 22:37
Jeremiah 23:5 . . . . Romans 1:3
Jeremiah 31:31–34. . . . . Hebrews 8:8–12; Hebrews
                                              10:16,17
Micah 4:2. . . . . Matthew 2:1; Luke 2:4–6
Micah 5:2–5 . . . . Matthew 2:5–6; John 7:42
Zechariah 9:9 . . . . Matthew 21:4,5; John 12:14,15
Zechariah 12:10 . . . . John 19:37
Malachi 3:1 . . . . Matthew 11:10; Mark 1:2; Luke
                                              7:27
Malachi 4:5,6 . . . . Matthew 11:13,14; Matthew
                                              17:10–13; Mark 9:11–13; Luke
                                              1:16,17

On Christmas Eve, as you light the white and last candle on your wreath, you may enjoy reading the Christmas story found in Luke 1:26–38 and Luke 2:1–20.

Christ, the Church's one foundation, is the cornerstone of our holidays, the centerpiece of our celebration.

May the peace that comes from knowing Christ the Lord be yours as you celebrate a year filled with happy holidays.

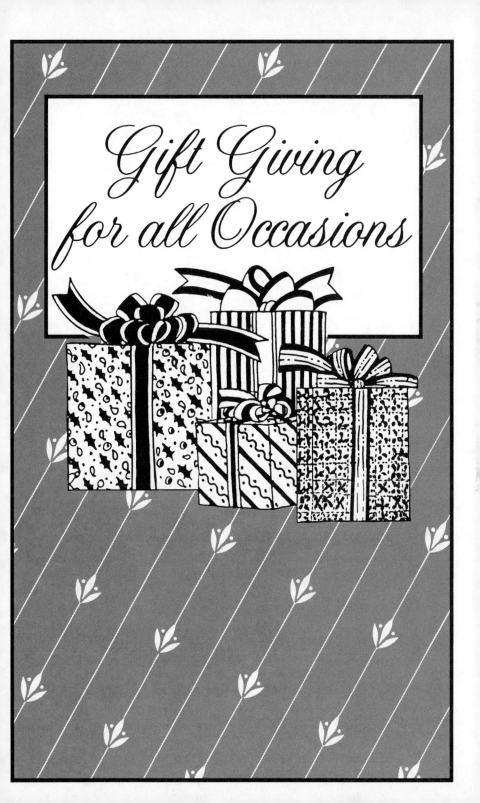

Gift Giving
for all Occasions

11

Gift Giving for All Occasions

Gift Wrapping for Gift Giving

Gift-giving goes on all year. It is one of the major parts of our lives. The love of giving gifts goes on and on and on throughout the year.

My friend Linda Risbrudt has been a real inspiration to me with her ideas on gift wrapping. Is your gift awkward in shape like a stuffed animal or potted plant? Plop it in a designer tote bag or shopping bag fluffed up with some colored tissue at the top, tie a bow on the handles and it's all wrapped up! How about several small gifts you are giving to one person? Toss them in a basket lined with tissue or fabric. Surround it with clear cellophane, tie a bow, and add a few silk or fresh flowers at the neck.

You can make your own gift wrap out of a variety of materials that are around the house at no cost. How about that plastic packing bubble sheet? Put some solid tissue paper underneath and wrap a gift in bubbles—especially for children. They love to open the gift and pop the bubbles.

Newspaper print makes great wrapping paper for the dad or friend who is into the stock market. Wrap the gift with the business section or stock market section. How about the travel or comic section? Tie a Garfield pencil or Snoopy notepad on top. Perhaps you've saved those little pieces of wrapping paper, thinking someday you would use them. Use them now! Simply tape together the pieces and make a patchwork gift wrap. Creative, original, and costs nothing.

Your plain paper or butcher paper can be used as a background for a rubber stamp, stickers, or vegetable prints. To make a potato print, cut a potato in half and carve a design into the potato—heart, angel, Christmas tree, teddy bear, bunny, etc. Dip the potato into acrylic paint thinned with water then stamp onto the brown paper. Thumbprint designs are unique and handprints are always fun. Have children color each print with a different color using crayons or felt tip pens. This is also a fun idea to use at a party for children or adults as an activity.

Collages can be made from pictures cut out of magazines and newspapers. These can be taped or glued to plain paper and used as a creative gift wrap.

You can wrap that baby gift in a disposable or cloth diaper. Tie the diaper with ribbon and add on diaper pins and baby powder. Talk about unique—you'll be the hit of the baby shower.

Paper napkins can be used as gift wrap in the theme colors for whatever occasion you are celebrating—green and red for Christmas; red, white, and pink for Valentine's Day, etc.

Wallpaper scraps make great wrappings for gifts or for covering boxes. Cute idea for the interior decorator.

Our son, Brad, works for a computer company and sells computers, so for birthdays and Christmas gifts we can use computer printout paper to wrap his gifts. It's nice to tie in the vocation with the gift wrap.

Kitchen gifts are adorable wrapped in a kitchen towel. Instead of a bow use a colored plastic or copper scouring pad. Colorful plastic measuring spoons are fun too! For the name tag use a wooden spoon and write the "To" and "From" on the handle with a felt pen.

Here's another different gift wrap idea for those on your list who like to travel. Just wrap their gift in a large colorful map and tie with a big ribbon.

At the after-Christmas supplies sales, you will find most gift wrap supplies marked down at least 50%. This is the time to pick up paper, ribbon, cards, tags, boxes, etc. A real relief of stress for next year.

Gift Tags

Making your own gift tags adds personality to any gift. A simple way is to use those small scraps of gift wrap and fold them to card size. Almost any object on which you can write or paint can be used as a tag: wooden spoons, ornaments, paper dolls, cookie dough cutters, key chains, shells, bookmarks, etc. Paint pens, which can be bought at craft stores, will write on almost anything and the color and print won't come off.

Tie-on's are a lot of fun and we've given you lots of ideas. Remember: If possible, capitalize on a hobby or vocation favorite for the person whose gift you are wrapping. For the golfer, use some golf tees tied onto the bow; an artist, a new brush; the mechanic, a new tool; the gardener, a new pair of gloves or seeds; the craft lady or knitter, knitting needles or embroidery thread tied onto the bow.

Here are some more package add-on ideas: Flowers—silk, real, or paper; leaves; pods; seeds; pinecones; nuts; a nosegay made out of doilies and flowers; evergreens; holly; mistletoe; bells; jingle bells; tree ornaments; sewing notions; spools of thread; batteries (especially on those gifts that will require them); office supplies for the secretary; school supplies for the student—pencils, pens, erasers; potpourri in lace bags tied with a bow.

Children will love this gift idea. Roll up a dollar bill (or more) and insert it into a balloon. Mail it along with a card and instructions to blow up the balloon and then pop it. Out comes the bill!

Gift Wrap Organization

Let's take the stress out of the gift wrapping and organize all the supplies we need to do the job—creatively and quickly.

The perfect tool to help that busy woman out of the gift wrapping dilemma is to have a "perfect gift wrap organizer." (This item can be purchased by mail order. Details at the end of this book.)

This organizer is the center of your wrapping experience and should include:

- Scissors
- Tape (double-stick for packages)
- Mailing tape—filament reinforced
- Wrapping papers: Rolled giftwrap is best—there are no seams and less waste. Solid colors—red, white, and green—give you more flexibility with ribbons, sticker art, and rubber stamping.
- Cellophane, clear
- Kraft paper—great for rubber stamping and sticker art.

Other Ideas

- Shelf paper
- Wallpaper
- Newspaper—funnies, sports page, stock market section, travel section
- Fabric
- Tissue paper—white (great for rubber stamping), colors, plain, pin-dot, graph, or patterned
- Gift boxes—enameled, fold-up, acrylic, or lucite
- Gift bags and totes—lunch bags, enamel bags, cellophane bags, window bags, small bottle and jar bags
- Tags or enclosure cards
- Ribbon—satin, plaid, taffeta, curling ribbon, curly satin, fabric, rickrack, shoelaces, measuring tape, lace, jute
- Stickers
- Mailing labels
- Glue gun, glue sticks
- Chenille stems—use on your make-ahead bows and store in a "perfect box"
- Rubber stamps, stamp pad, or brush markers.

Hints for Use of Old Wrapping Paper and Bows

- Make used wrapping paper new again by lightly spraying the wrong side with spray starch and press with a warm iron.

- Run wrinkled ribbon through a hot curling iron to take out old creases.
- Ribbons—make your own with pieces of leftover fabric. Almost any type of fabric can be cut to the desired width and length. Striped materials are great to cut into even widths. Then press between sheets of wax paper with a hot iron. This will keep the strips from unraveling and provides enough stiffness for the ribbon to hold its shape when making it into a bow.

More Wrapping Ideas

Cellophane

- For those "How am I going to wrap that?" gifts. It will always get you out of a jam.
- For a basket, bucket, pail, or small wagon toy filled with goodies—tie it with a fluffy bow and a sprig of holly or pine or use stickers.
- For your gifts of food—cookies on a Christmas plate; breads wrapped with cellophane and Christmas ribbon; a homemade quiche; a basket of muffins in a checked napkin or muffins in a muffin tin.
- For a plant.
- For fresh bouquet of flowers—tied with a beautiful bow and a special note inside.

Gift Bags

A wonderful idea for a quick, easy and decorative way to wrap! They are reusable too!

Line bag with contrasting tissue or wrap your gift item or items in tissue. Add a bow to the handle with a gift tag. Add shredded tissue (Tissue Toss) on top for a festive look. (Use any color combination depending on the time of the year and cut into

¼″ strips—then toss like a green salad and you've made "tissue toss.")

Decorate bag with stickers, banners, or cutouts from old Christmas cards.

Large silver or black or green plastic garbage bags may be "just the thing" to hide a large gift. Add a banner, large bow, and stickers. It will look just like Santa's pack.

Reuse your bags for lunches or to hold your needlework.

Gift Boxes and Containers

- The decorated ones need only a ribbon! Always get a courtesy box, tissue, and ribbon whenever you buy anything at a department store or where the gift wrap is free. Save them in your gift wrap center for the times you need them. Usually they fold flat and are easy to store.
- Wrap a lid separate from the bottom to use again and again.
- Use tins, ceramic containers, lucite or acrylic boxes, flowerpots, buckets, pails, and baskets.

Gift Certificates

- Purchase from stores
- Make your own with calligraphy, sticker art, or rubber stamp art and then laminate them. Have certificates redeemable for:

Babysitting	Day of shopping
Dinners in your home	& lunch
Frozen yogurt	Trip to the zoo
Plays	

Gift Boxes

Below are diagrams for four basic bows which you can make: the basic bow, the pompon bow, the looped bow, and the tailored tie bow. You can get a different feel by using different widths of ribbons.

Basic Bow

It helps to have a small helper to hold a finger on this bow while you tie it to the package, but it's not absolutely necessary!

1. Wind ribbon or yarn around a piece of cardboard or around your hand until you have the fullness you desire. (See Diagram 1.)

2. Carefully remove the wound ribbon or yarn, pinching the center together. Using the ties on the package, tie the bow in the middle, leaving longer ends as streamers if desired. (See Diagram 2.)

3. If you used ribbed ribbon, curl the streamers by pulling the blade of a pair of scissors along the length of the ribbon as shown in Diagram 3.

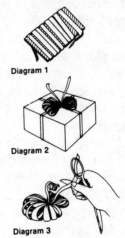

Diagram 1

Diagram 2

Diagram 3

Pompon Bow

These bows are expensive when purchased but easy to make after just a little practice.

1. To make a pompon bow, wrap the ribbon in circles as shown in Diagram 1.

2. Flatten and fold the ribbon and cut diagonal wedges in the center as shown in Diagram 2.

3. Tie the center as shown in Diagram 3.

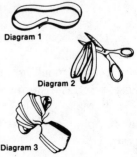

Diagram 1

Diagram 2

Diagram 3

4. Pull out the loops and fluff the bow as shown in Diagram 4.

5. Attach the bow to the package with double-faced tape or a piece of regular tape rolled into a circle.

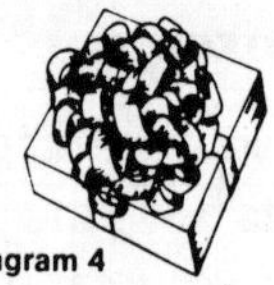

Diagram 4

Looped Bow

These bows are attractive and easy to make.

1. First decide how many loops to make in your bow. The more loops, the grander the final effect.

2. Make the first loop and secure it in place with tape as shown in Diagram 1. If you are using satin ribbon that adheres to itself, moisten the ribbon where you want the loops to be joined.

Diagram 1

3. Keep making loops until you feel the bow is complete. Fasten all the loops together with a staple or tape. (See Diagram 2.)

Diagram 2

4. For variety, make several looped bows and arrange them attractively on the top of the package as shown in Diagram 3. Attach them to the package with double-faced tape.

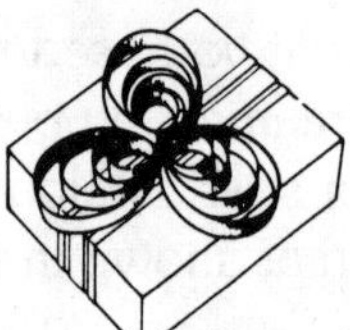

Diagram 3

Tailored Tie Bow

These bows are as easy to make as the looped bows and travel beautifully . . . use them on all those Christmas packages you have to mail! Very wide ribbon is especially pretty in this bow design and is a stunning way to adorn a large package.

1. Make one large loop and tape overlapping ends together. (See Diagram 1.)

Diagram 1

146

2. Make a smaller loop and lay it on the top of the first loop. Staple or tape both loops together. (See Diagram 2.)

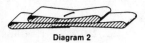

Diagram 2

3. Two loops are enough to achieve the effect of the tailored tie bow, but, depending on the size of your first loop, you may want to use three or four layers of loops in descending sizes. Once you have as many loops as desired, cut a small piece of ribbon to wrap around the center. Secure it on the back of the bow with tape as shown in Diagram 3. Use double-faced tape to attach the bow to the package.

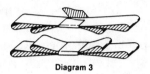

Diagram 3

With very little effort our packages can look as lovely on the outside as the wonderful things they contain on the inside.

Gift Ideas for Christmas and All Occasions

For the person who sews there are endless ideas, but what about the person who doesn't or has no time or interest? We've attempted to give you a good balance of ideas. The most important tool you'll need is a hot glue gun. Invest this year and you'll have it for years to come. Regular glue will not do the job that a hot glue gun will.

1. *Stockings*—I've filled stockings for each member of the family since they were babies and still do even though they're grown adults. I've included razors, shampoo, hose, undies, toys, books, crazy glue, flashlights, screwdrivers, nail polish and remover, stationery, make-up items, coupons, gift certificates, measuring spoons, tapes, and so on. It can get expensive, but I start early in the year and toss items into a storage box. By December my box is filled and it's so much fun for me to go through it and

divide the items up. It's never too early to start saving stocking stuffers.

2. *Books*—Books make a gift that goes on and on for every occasion: Christian comic books for the junior age; Bibles; children's Bibles; storybooks; teaching, how-to, and inspirational books.

3. *Panties*—One mom sewed red and green lace on little girls' panties. When her children are babies they can wear the panties over their diapers for the holiday, and then later they'll wear them as regular panties.

4. *Photo albums*—Photo albums can be covered with fabric. There are patterns in craft books and fabric pattern books. These can be done completely with a glue gun.

5. *Glue gun*—You can glue bows and other decorations on the tree, packages, walls, wreaths, plaques, flower arrangements, glass, wood, fabric, metal, cotton or tags. You can purchase this wonderful item at hardware stores, craft shops, hobby shops, and sometimes even at the drugstore.

6. *Tins*—Coffee tins can be covered with felt, fabric, or wrapping paper. These make great containers for gift items. They can be filled with pencils, erasers, a small notepad, small stapler, hole punch, glue, rubber bands, rubber stamp and stamp pad, stickers, stamps, and stationery.

Coffee tins are great for baking in, too. Simply fill the container two-thirds full with your favorite muffin or bread mix and bake. Let cool about ten minutes. If the baked item doesn't pop right out, open the other end and push the loaf through. This makes a round loaf and looks pretty cut on a plate.

These tins can also be used in the car for emergency rips, tears, or lost buttons. Fill the container with needles, thread, small scissors, buttons, measuring tape, glue, lace, and ribbon.

Fill another tin with first-aid items and give as a gift for use in a car, boat, or motor home.

Fill a two- or three-pound tin with baby items. Cover the tin with baby fabric using your glue gun and fill with sample sizes of powder, lotion, wipes, Vaseline, pins, disposable diaper, rattle, etc.

Another idea is to fill a tin for the gardener in the family with seeds, gloves, insect spray, etc.

For college students or a child's camping trip, fill with shampoo, hair spray, comb, small brush, toothpaste, toothbrush, insect repellent, etc. We can go on and on. Use your imagination.

7. *Boxes and other containers*—The following are some ideas for items that can be put into one of our "perfect boxes" that has been covered with fabric. They could also be put into plastic buckets, paint pails, or plastic carryalls. One of these could be filled with auto emergency tools such as jumper cables, a towel, first-aid kit, flares, fire extinguisher, and hide-a-key case.

For the fishing nut, fill with hooks, line, and bait. The traveler could use road maps and a campsite information book. These types of practical gifts are always well-received and well-used.

We all love home-baked items because these are an expression of love. Put your food items in tote bags, plastic baggies, jars, or decorator sacks. One mom gave chocolate chip cookies to each of her children's teachers in a brown lunch sack. She then rubber-stamped chocolate chip cookies all over the outside of the bag. It was adorable and yet so simple.

8. *Nightshirt*—One of the cutest gift ideas I've seen came in the form of a gift. It was a nightshirt made from a man's white T-shirt. You need to sew for this idea. Purchase an extra-large white T-shirt, preferably V-neck. Sew white eyelet lace around the sleeves, bottom, and neck. Down the front, sew more lace, about two to four rows and top it off with a small satin bow at the middle of the neck. This can be the hit of any gift exchange. One mom made them for all her four daughters and used red and green eyelet lace for their Christmas nightshirts.

9. *Garden glove puppets*—This is one of our grandchildren's favorites. Gardening gloves are very inexpensive. With some pom-poms and plastic eyes or buttons, you can create Old MacDonald and four farm animals. A Christ-centered puppet can also be made with Joseph, Mary, Baby Jesus, a donkey, and the innkeeper. You glue these on the tips of the glove fingers—one for each character. Each glove can illustrate a different story.

10. *Christmas decorations*—These make great gifts for

anytime during the year. Our daughter received a wedding gift of a Christmas tablecloth, Christmas print napkins, several ornaments, and a set of red-and-green candles. A perfect gift for a new couple to use for their first Christmas.

11. *Walnuts and rice*—This gift makes a real impact. I share it in my seminars and the women all want a copy of the recipe:

> This jar contains 25 walnuts and 2½ cups of rice. The walnuts represent the things God would have us to do and the rice represents the fun things that we like to do. If you pour the rice into the jar first, the walnuts will never fit. If you put the walnuts in the jar first, the rice poured over and around the nuts fit just fine.
>
> The lesson of course is if we put time with God and for God before time for other things we want to do, we'll have plenty of time for both.
>
> If, however, we put the things we want to do first, we'll never fit time for God into our life.

Find any quart-size jar. Put into the jar 25 whole walnuts in the shell. Pour over the walnuts 2½ cups of rice. You can decorate the lid or tie a bow around the jar and attach the recipe. I have mine in the kitchen and I continually get comments.

12. *Jar hats*—I love to decorate my jars and make hats for them. I can use scrap fabrics of all kinds. I then fill my jars with homemade jams, spice tea mix, mocha coffee mix, beans, flour, oatmeal, etc.

To make jar hats, cut a circle from some cloth—a plate will do for a pattern. For a gallon-size jar, use a 10″ plate; for a wide-mouth quart jar, use a 9″-diameter plate; for a regular-size quart jar, use a 7″-diameter plate. Turn the edge under and sew narrow lace around the outside of the circle. On the wrong side of the fabric draw a circle on the fabric where the elastic will be placed. While pulling the elastic tight, sew it on the hat with a zigzag stitch. Turn the hat to the right side and fill with fiberfill or cotton balls. Place it on the jar and tie a ribbon around the gathered part to complete the hat.

13. *Dusting mitt*—Our granddaughter, Christine, loves to help her Grammie around the house. She also loves farm animals, so I purchased a commercial car-washing mitt at a variety store. With squares of felt I cut out a cute pig (see Exhibit H). You could use a white athletic sock if you can't find the car mitt. These are great gifts for preschoolers.

14. *Place mats*—I've found heavy-duty plastic oval-shaped place mats on sale in a variety of colors and designs. Here's an idea for gifts to give to a family. Take your paint pen (black preferably) and draw on each one where the plate, silverware, glass, and salad plate goes (see Exhibit I). Parents love this gift because the children get excited about setting the table by themselves and it teaches them how to properly set the table. Remember, the sharp edge of the knife looks at the plate. You can add to this gift napkins and napkin rings.

15. *Pillow*—This is unusual and personal. Paint a pillow with non-toxic acrylic paints or a paint pen. List your friend's important personal dates and places on it or perhaps his or her favorite Bible verse. Children's and/or grandchildren's names can be put on along with their handprints.

16. *Gift wrap*—Practical, you bet! Give a gift of all-occasion wrap with ribbon, bows, scissors, tape, and tags. This will be appreciated by just about anyone.

17. *Memory plate*—We have a very exciting tradition in our family that also makes a beautiful gift. It's an "Occasion To Remember" plate and is used to build self-esteem, memories, and tradition. We only have one, but we use it often.

With a paint pen we record the memory on the back of the plate and date it. We've even asked our guests to autograph the plate. They always feel honored and special.

Here's what one mom wrote about how they used their plate:

> We have just moved to San Juan Capistrano from Ft. Worth, Texas. We have two beautiful sons, Kevin is 18 and Dwayne is 14. Kevin has had a very difficult time adjusting, mostly because he is in his senior year in high school. His temperament is melancholy. Four days after attending your seminar and purchasing the "Blue Plate" our oldest son tried to commit suicide. This is a young man who has been known for his stand for Christ, a leader among Christian kids in church and school. Kevin was in the hospital a couple of days and on his return home with us we used the beautiful "Blue Plate." This was the first time we had used it and now the boys ask to use it. The best surprise for me was the morning our youngest son served me breakfast in bed with our "Blue Plate." This plate never sits at our table without my thinking of two very special people who love our Lord enough to be open to His guidance in sharing their happiness and lives with others. God Bless you both.

18. *Christmas plate*—Several years ago our dear friends Dave and Joan Marriner gave to us a lovely Christmas plate filled with her special homemade cookies and candy. We were thrilled with the food, but better yet they said the plate was ours, too. The next year they repeated the gift with another Christmas plate of a different design. Every year we have received a new and different Christmas plate and now we have a lovely plate collec-

tion to use all during the holidays.

19. *Coupon books*—These can be made out of colored construction paper. Cut the paper approximately 3½" x 7½". Print "To" and "Good For" on it.

Here are some ideas for your coupon book:

• Take out the trash for five days without complaints
• Wash windows with smiles
• Bathe dog without a mess
• Mow lawn or weed garden
• Cook a meal
• Breakfast in bed

20. *Barrettes*—All little girls love barrettes. To make them special, glue decorative strands of ribbon to the top side of the barrette. At the ends of the ribbon, tie small pinecones, feathers, beads, or jingle bells.

21. *Doorstop*—Fill an old quart-size mason jar with pretty pebbles or seashells and tie a ribbon around the top.

TO: _____
THIS COUPON ENTITLES YOU TO A BATCH OF
YOUR FAVORITE CHRISTMAS COOKIES. (IF
YOU'LL HELP DECORATE THEM.)
SIGNED: _____

Note: You can photocopy coupons, then color them in.

22. *Magazine subscription*—Avoid last-minute embarrassment when you've forgotten a gift. Simply wrap up an issue of a magazine and attach a tag saying a subscription is on the way. Don't forget to follow through.

God has designed each of us uniquely and creatively as women. We are the ones who set the thermostats in our homes. What we do today will be tomorrow's memories.

As each holiday approaches around the year, let's look to God to motivate us to build memories. Take the time to make the family occasion special. Draw in each member to help create the memory. What an opportunity to teach our children and grandchildren the importance of family holiday time. It can be a time of family healing and forgiving all because you committed to make holidays special.

This book has given you the tool and plan to make it happen. Now work the plan and God will honor your heart and the plan will work for you. Your holiday will become an event that will be passed on from generation to generation. May you be the one to set that temperature to a warm and loving spirit that others will want to have and experience as you create those joy-filled and joyful holidays.

"More Hours In My Day" can provide many of the organizational materials that are recommended in this book. You may obtain a price list or seminar information by sending your request and a self-addressed, stamped envelope to:

MORE HOURS IN MY DAY
2838 Rumsey Drive
Riverside, California 92506

Exhibits

SHOPPER'S GUIDE

NAME	GIFT/ ALTERNATE	SIZE	STORE	COST BUDGET	COST ACTUAL

EXHIBIT A

GIFTS GIVEN			
OCCASION	TO	GIFT	YEAR

GIFTS RECEIVED

GIFT	OCCASION	TO	FROM	THANK YOU

EXHIBIT C

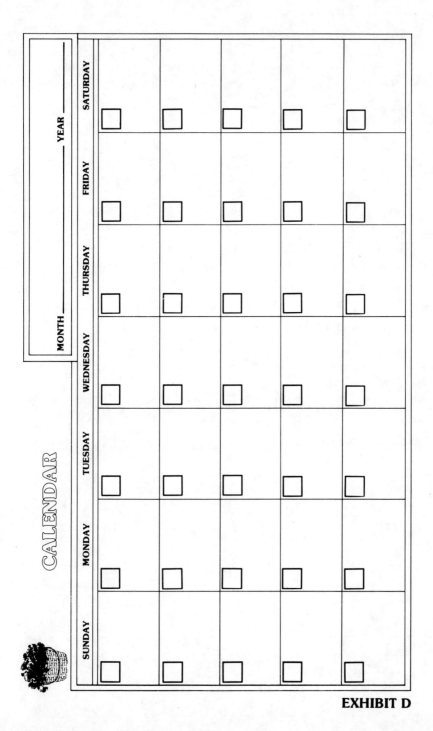

EXHIBIT D

HOSPITALITY SHEET

Date: _____ Place: _____
Time: _____ Number of Guests: _____
Event: _____ Theme: _____

Things to Do	✔	Menu	Preparation Time
One Week Before:		Appetizers:	
Three Days Before:		Entree:	
One Day Before:		Side Dishes:	
Day Of:		Salad:	
		Dessert:	
Last Minute:		Drinks:	

Guest List	RSVP		Notes	Supplies
	Yes	No		
				Tables/Chairs
				Dishes
				Silver
				Glasses
				Centerpiece

EXHIBIT E

CHRISTMAS CARD RECORD

NAME	ADDRESS	YEAR	SENT	REC'D

EXHIBIT F

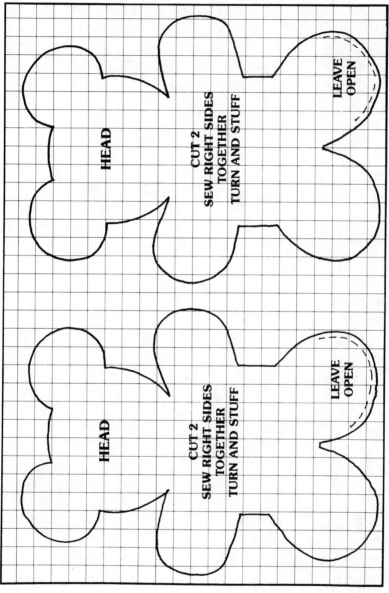

EXHIBIT G

To enlarge: Duplicate square by square to a larger size grid. The grid for one bear is 22 squares down and 16 squares wide. Determine grid size by dividing desired bear height by 22. For example: a 5½" bear uses a ¼" grid, a 22" bear uses a 1" grid, etc.

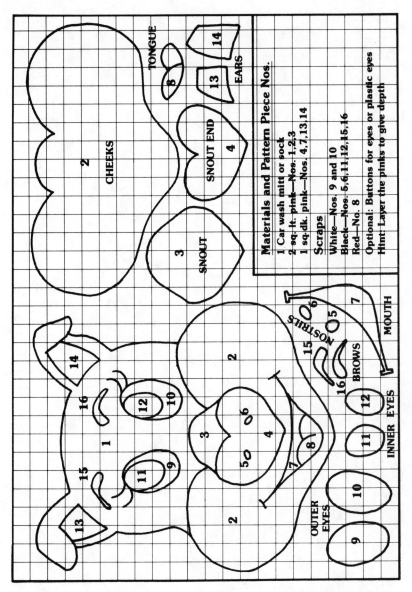

EXHIBIT H

To enlarge: Duplicate square by square to a larger size grid. The grid for this design is 22 squares down and 16 squares wide. Determine grid size by dividing desired height by 22.

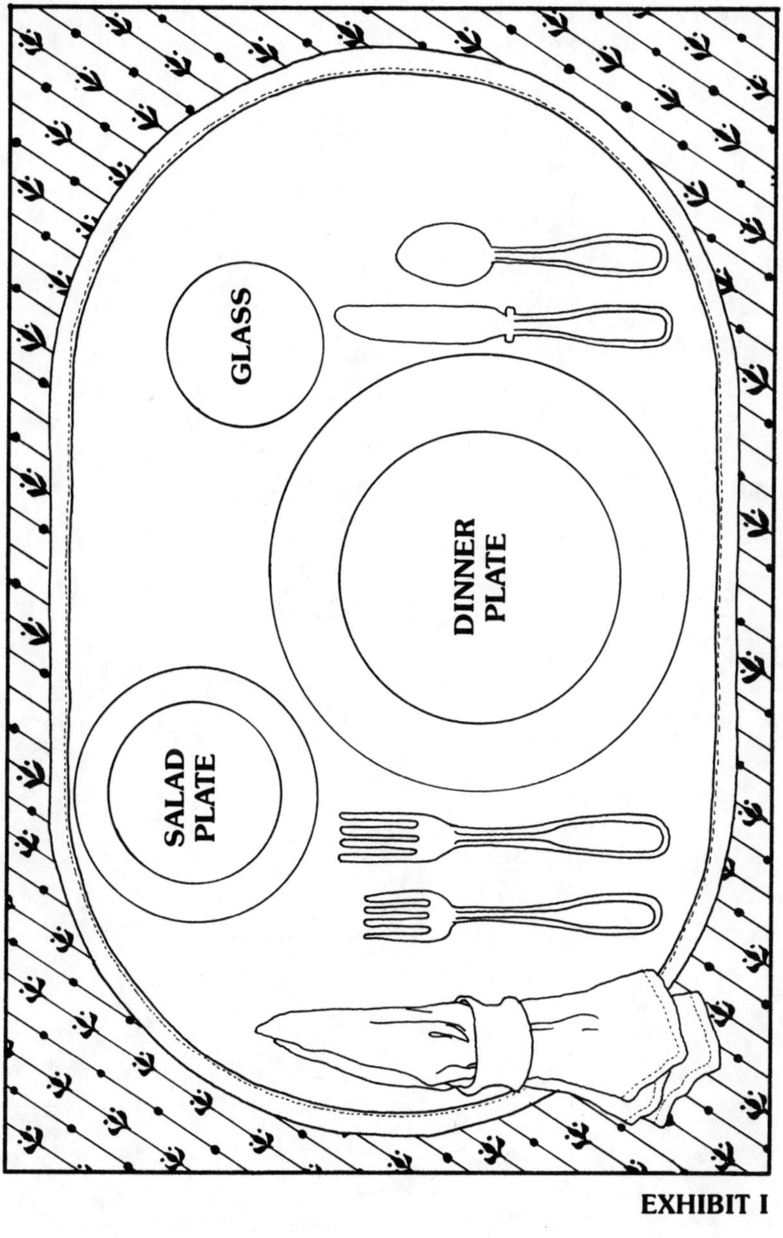
GLASS
DINNER PLATE
SALAD PLATE

EXHIBIT I